I want to talk about Kick." Jason said.

"Sorry about the other night. He can be so funny, or he can be so obnoxious."

Jason ignored the apology. "He's no good for you, Maddy."

"You have no right to say so. You don't even know him."

"He's going to make you fall—if you haven't already."

"Like you should care! Besides, you don't think I have any place to fall from. Remember? I'm a liar about my faith because I dress funny."

"Listen. I've been watching how he treats you. He puts you down in subtle ways. I've heard him make fun of your humor, your personality, your clothes, your weight—and you aren't even close to being overweight!" Jason suddenly blushed and looked away.

"He's only joking," Maddy half-protested. She'd always secretly wondered if he *was* joking.

Jason regained his composure. "If he's joking, how come your face gets a hurt look? And how come his voice changes to a snarl when he says it?"

"It's his way of being funny." Even to Maddy, the defense sounded weak.

NUMBER 2

HOMEWARD HEART

BY LISSA HALLS JOHNSON

HOMEWARD HEART
published by Palisades
a part of the Questar publishing family

© 1996 by Lissa Halls Johnson
International Standard Book Number: 0-88070-948-0

Cover photography by Mike Houska
Cover designed by Kevin Keller

Printed in the United States of America

For information:
QUESTAR PUBLISHERS, INC.
POST OFFICE BOX 1720
SISTERS, OREGON 97759

96 97 98 99 00 01 02 03 — 10 9 8 7 6 5 4 3 2 1

For Linnea Holmlund

My daughter,
My sister,
My friend.

The LORD does not look at the things man looks at.
Man looks at the outward appearance, but
the LORD looks at the heart.

1 SAMUEL 16:7b

PROLOGUE

OCTOBER...

Maddy MacDonald pedaled her beat-up bike to the top of the hill on the north side of Pacific Cascades University. In the eight weeks she'd been in Seattle, her leg muscles had grown stronger, but they still ached by the time she reached the top. At least she didn't have to walk her bike up all the hills any more.

She really didn't have to go this way to get to her new job at Starbucks on Pill Hill. This wild speed ride, she had decided, would be the best way to celebrate the fact that she'd finally landed a job. The school had promised to provide a position through their work-study program when one opened up. Until then, this job was more than a fill-in. It was a blessing from heaven.

Starting on level ground, Maddy pedaled as fast as she could. The hill dropped beneath her, and she hunkered down over the handlebars as if she were ducking under low branches. *Yes!* screamed her heart. *Yes!* The wind tore at her eyes, bringing tears. Her hair whipped behind her, red and wild. The rushing wind surrounded her, deafened her.

She closed her eyes to savor the sensation. Her bike wobbled from the speed. A moment later, Maddy opened her eyes again just in time to see that she was blowing the stop sign at the crux of a Y intersection. As she flew forward, a blur and a roar came from the other branch of the Y. Moving fast, she swerved to the left and her bike fell beneath her, depositing her in a skidding, crumpled heap.

Without a thought to her own scrapes and bruises, Maddy untangled herself from the bike frame and flew across the street to where a motorcycle and rider lay in a growing puddle of gas and oil.

"Oh, God, please don't let him be hurt. Jesus, I'm sorry. Oh, God, what have I done?" she mumbled as she ran to the downed biker. He climbed to his knees and removed his helmet, then stood and shook his head as if to clear it. The moment he caught sight of Maddy, his face twisted in disbelief.

"I'm so sorry," Maddy said earnestly. "Oh, are you okay? Please tell me you're okay."

"What did you think you were doing back there?" he shouted. "Do stop signs not apply to you for some insane reason?"

"I'm so sorry. I didn't expect…I mean, I really thought…."

"You were *thinking*?"

"Are you hurt?" she said, reaching out to touch the arm that he held close to his chest.

"I'm fine," he snapped, jerking it away. "Nice mouth, by the way. I could hear you swearing all the way across the street."

"What?" Maddy said, feeling puzzled. "No! You misunderstood. I wasn't swearing. I don't swear any more. I gave it up. I was *praying*. I was scared you were really hurt."

He had turned away from her and was trying in vain to lift the damaged bike. He stopped and stared at Maddy. "You pray?" he asked, clearly not believing her.

She nodded. "I do. All the time. I'm a Christian."

He looked her up and down, taking in her short white top, her long gauzy Indian-print skirt, her ankle-high lace-up boots. He especially stopped to study the dainty silver chain that hung around her waist, and draped through a tiny navel ring. "You can't possibly be a Christian."

"And why not?" Maddy replied, her hands on her slender hips.

"Dressed like that," he said, waving vaguely at her, "I don't think so."

"God loves me just the way I am," Maddy replied. She cocked her head. "How do you think I should dress?"

He ran a hand through his tousled brown hair. His brown eyes scanned a handful of onlookers gathered on the sidewalk. "Like that," he said, pointing to a very clean-cut looking girl who wore loose jeans and a sweatshirt.

"If I looked like that you would think I was a Christian?" Maddy asked.

"You'd at least *look* like one," he answered.

"Well," Maddy said, more than a little miffed. "Thanks for the fashion advice, but I'm late for my first day of work. Since you seem okay, I'm going to take off. Maybe someone who meets your dress-code standards can help you with your bike."

She hopped back on her bike and rode away, pedaling as fast as her legs would take her. Her hands shook, both from anger and from the shock of a near accident. "That creep," she muttered. "I sure hope I never run into him again."

The joke hit her, and she threw back her head and laughed.

1

Maddy approached the enormous building with great anticipation. Finally, her work-study assignment had come through. She had told the office she'd take the first available job, no matter what it was. She had assured them that she learned quickly and promised she'd put her whole heart into it. In return, they unwittingly placed her in a situation that would, at the very least, prove to be interesting. Upon hearing her assignment, Maddy did not breathe a word about the fact that she was somewhat unfamiliar with libraries. She didn't want to lose the chance to earn the desperately needed money that would keep her at PCU.

She took the concrete steps two at a time. On the front of the ivy-covered brick building was a sign that read, simply, LIBRARY. It looked as though another plate had formerly hung above it, but gaping holes in the bricks indicated that something had happened to it.

At the top of the stairs, Maddy pulled off her hood, shook her Irish red hair, and reached for the twisted handles of iron, anxious to throw open the doors to her new adventure. She paused as her eyes caught a rare glimpse of the Seattle sun starting to break through the clouds. Maddy checked her watch. She had a few minutes to spare. She moved toward a concrete arm that jutted out from the building, providing a border for the steps and a perfect place from which to survey the campus. Maddy sat, hugging her knees to her chest, soaking up the sun.

November 1. How fitting that I should start a new job right at the time of year that's always brought change for my family. Maddy almost laughed at using the term "family" to describe the people who had been a part of her upbringing. Sure, she had the typical family figures in her life: mother, father, and two siblings. What wasn't typical was how they lived.

Maddy's father earned his living by drawing charcoal and chalk portraits of people in malls. Her mother found odd jobs —mostly in the malls—to help pay the few bills they had. They moved from city to city, always considering the number of malls within a fifty-mile radius. Sometimes they stayed in one place for a full year, but most of the time they moved every four to six months. Maddy didn't mind the moves. They were an adventure. New friends. New weather. New schools. New everything. Her dad especially liked to move at the beginning of November, because that was just before the Christmas season began. The best time for portraits.

Her parents were so wrapped up in their jobs, they were hardly ever home, leaving Maddy and her sisters to fend for themselves. That hadn't seemed so terrible, either. But lately, Maddy had been feeling that she'd missed out on the family thing. She had always been on her own; now she wanted something more. Some kind of connection.

She sighed. There wasn't time for any kind of musing right now. She'd hate to lose her chance at this job just because she couldn't peel herself away from the sun and her thoughts.

Getting up, she brushed off the damp seat of her skirt. She reached to open the library doors, which had been constructed from solid oak and were carved with the images of roaring lions, flowers, leaves, and scrolls. She paused and let her fingers dance lightly over the carvings. One thing her father had taught her was an appreciation for the artistic efforts of others. And this artist definitely deserved appreciation. Promising herself to look at the carvings more closely at another time, Maddy shifted into her practical mode and pulled hard on the door.

A breath of warm air rushed past and collided with the moist, cold air of Seattle. The scent that blew in her face was one that Maddy had seldom encountered. She closed her eyes to inhale and savor.

Opening her eyes a moment later, she stepped farther into the library, where she discovered rows and rows of books. Endless rows that stretched farther than she could see. Column after column of books, reaching to the ceiling. At one point, Maddy could see a glimpse of the floors above, which also were overflowing with books. Maddy looked around in wonder. *This isn't like the high school libraries I've been in. What have I been missing?*

Chills tingled through her. She couldn't help smiling. She'd only been a Christian for nine months. But this God she met had done an exceedingly abundant thing again. Her smile grew bigger, as if she had a wild and wonderful secret—*I'm going to get paid to be here!*

Trying to walk quietly didn't work at all. With each step, her lace-up boots clicked loudly against the marble floor. Maddy looked around nervously. When no one seemed to pay any attention, she exhaled. That's when she noticed the other sounds: whispers, footsteps, rustling pages. Yet around the sounds, there was also silence. Without thinking, Maddy wrapped her arms around herself, feeling an odd sense of belonging. She wanted to belong somewhere, or to someone. The adventures of her life—which she cherished—had kept her alive and thinking and excited, but *belonging* wasn't a part of her past experience.

Maddy moved confidently across the vast floor toward the curved desk that dominated the marble entry. Several people bustled around behind it. A tiny, wrinkled lady glanced up from her desk and smiled. "May I help you?" The woman touched one hand to her graying hair, which was pulled back into a bun.

"I'm on work-study," Maddy told her in a whisper. "I'm here to replace the girl who had to leave school?" She blushed when she realized she had finished her sentence in a question. Bad habit from forever ago.

"Oh, yes! What's your name?"

"Maddy. Maddy MacDonald."

"Maddy." She stuck out a tiny weathered hand. "I'm Alma." Maddy put her hand in Alma's, feeling the old skin slip across her hand, and smiled. Maddy liked her immediately. Alma was one of the few people who didn't stare at her stomach as though she were some kind of freak. So what if she decided to pierce her navel and wear a silver ring through it? You'd think she was some kind of alien the way people stared at times.

"We have a fellow here who has been with us since just

before school started," Alma said in a loud practiced whisper. "I'll have him show you around." She winked. "He's a good-looking guy, too. Reminds me of James Dean. I'll go find him."

After Alma had disappeared, Maddy turned to look about her. She leaned back on the counter and gazed at the domed ceiling, feeling the stretch all the way down her spine. *You're home,* a voice inside her seemed to say.

I don't have a home, she reminded the voice.

Alma must have perfected the silent-walking thing because Maddy didn't even hear her return. What caught her attention was a stifled gasp.

Maddy spun around, wearing a welcoming smile to greet her co-worker. But rather than seeing the welcome reflected in another's eyes, Maddy was met with a narrow glare. "Hey, aren't you—?" she started to say, her mind registering recognition.

"Jason," Alma said, without looking at him, "this is Maddy, your new co-worker. I'd like you to show her around and teach her what we expect."

Maddy reached out her hand to Jason. He ignored the gesture.

Alma looked quizzically at him. "Jason! I thought you were a gentleman."

Jason opened his mouth, then closed it. He reached for Maddy's hand and held it—a little too tightly.

"You're here until five?" Alma asked.

Maddy nodded.

"Say good-bye on your way out." Alma touched Maddy's arm and returned to her desk.

They stood there, seemingly intent on staring one another down.

"This is the library," Jason said a moment later with a wave of his hand. "Put books away and help students find what they need." He turned and walked swiftly toward a row of books.

Maddy clenched her teeth. Shaking her head, she sighed. Her boots clicked quickly across the floor, her nineteen silver bracelets jangling with her every move.

Without turning around, Jason stopped. With a slow, forced-control pivot, he faced her. "What?" he asked.

Maddy tilted her head and smiled. "Maybe I'm not the smartest person you've ever worked with. But I'll bet there are a few things you left out of your instructions." She gave him that smile again, hoping he'd ease up.

No such luck. Jason couldn't be moved by her smile or any other feminine wile she might try on him. "You're a freshman in college, right?"

She nodded.

"Then figure it out."

"I've never really been in a library like this before."

A look of disbelief swept across his face, followed by a flash of compassion. If Maddy had been a less observant person, she would have missed the whole show of emotion. It took the zing out of her rising anger.

Jason opened his mouth as if to say something, then looked away. Maddy wished she knew what was going through his brain. She had seen him around school several times since her clash with him and his motorcycle. She thought he was incredibly good looking for such a clean-cut kid. He looked like he walked through cornfields and plucked the heads off wheat.

But Alma was right. He also had that James Dean rebel look

about him when he rode his bike. Cool. Clear-headed. Goal-oriented. Solid. He looked like Maddy felt. She envied him his motorcycle. If she had the bucks, she'd buy one in an instant. She didn't want to sit on the back of one. She wanted to be in front. In control. Feeling the wind in her face, the power beneath her, in front of her, compelling her, driving her forward to meet life head on.

Maddy didn't move. Jason began to move silently toward an open cart laden with books. His face seemed to reflect an inner turmoil. His eyes flickered. His jaw clenched, then relaxed.

She followed—not so silently—yet kept her distance.

"This is what you do," he said so softly she almost didn't hear him. He certainly didn't look her direction. Jason picked up several of the books and headed toward her. He placed the books in various places on the shelf, then returned to the cart.

Maddy had to swallow her laughter. She could tell her very presence irritated this guy. He tried to pretend he didn't know she was there, but she knew he was aware of her as each minute ticked by.

She'd met so many types of people in her mobile life, she didn't know if there were any new ones left to meet. She'd learned to read them pretty well. And this cross between a farm boy and a jock was no idiot. He moved about the library as though it were his sole possession. He touched the books as though caressing his dearest love.

Maddy decided later that she especially liked watching when students sought his assistance. He spoke to them with eagerness and anticipation. He didn't treat them as if they were intruders. As he moved away from Maddy in his quest to help

16

the students, she didn't follow him…except with her eyes.

She stayed near the cart, knowing he would return to it like a homing pigeon. The cart part of his job seemed easy enough. Take a book with a number on its spine and find corresponding numbers on the shelves. Stash it, then get the next one.

Without being asked, she began to shelve books while he was away helping another student. She moved more quickly than he and was shelving one of the last books when Jason returned.

"What do you think you are doing?" He sounded panicked.

She smiled. "I suppose I'm doing the job I was paid to do. You told me to figure it out, so I've done that."

Jason went to the shelf. "You're doing it all wrong! Why don't you just go away and find some job in the Pizza Den? Or better yet, how about Madam Kuzinka's Palm Reading and Fortune Telling?"

Without thinking, Maddy laughed.

"That wasn't supposed to be funny," Jason said, sounding disappointed.

"Look," Maddy said, her humor gone. "I'm going to work here, whether you like it or not. I'm going to learn how to do things one way or another. If you don't teach me right, and I learn them wrong, you'll get blamed for doing a shoddy job. If you decide to teach me, I'll learn quickly, do a good job, stay out of your hair, and everyone will think you are a marvelous trainer. What's it going to be?" Maddy stared at him with her intense, Irish green eyes.

Jason looked at her still, his hardened square jaw mirroring his attitude.

"Fine." Maddy picked up another book and shelved it.

"Stop it!" Jason said, yanking the book off the shelf. "You can't just put them any old place."

"I'm putting them on the shelf according to the little numbers on the back."

"It's called a spine," Jason said without thinking. "And you can't just shove them up there." His face registered the concern of a teacher. Just what Maddy wanted. "They have to go alphabetically by the author's last name within the numbers. And if there's more than one book by the same author, the titles are alphabetized."

"Ahh, Master Jason. You have taught me well." Maddy bowed low from the waist, and took another book. She popped it on the shelf, then stood back and gestured like a game-show assistant, pointing toward a vowel on a great lighted board.

Her quick eyes caught Jason stifling a smile. "Yeah," he conceded. "That's right."

Maybe this guy isn't hopeless after all.

He pushed the cart at her and said. "Okay, smarty pants. Finish this cart."

"Smarty pants?" Maddy laughed. "I haven't heard someone say that in…." Her voice trailed off as she realized he was making a hasty retreat.

Maddy started to ponder the reasons for Jason's rude behavior, but her thoughts quickly became consumed by a book that caught her attention. She opened it, skimmed the words, then glanced at the inside flap of the back cover. There she found a picture of the author.

She put the book in its place on the shelf and opened a second. On the back flap, she found another photo. This guy was downright ugly. Maddy couldn't help but wonder about these people. *Who would actually write a book? How could they come up with that many words?*

She opened more and more books. Lots of them had photos of authors. Not many of them looked like what society would call normal or glamorous. The brief descriptions beneath snagged her attention. She read every one.

"What are you doing?" Jason's loud whisper startled her. She didn't answer, just stared at him.

"You're supposed to be working," Jason said.

"This is fascinating," Maddy replied, holding up the book.

Jason seemed to be stifling a smile again. "Fascinate yourself on your own time."

"Really, Jason. How can you work fast when there is so much here? I never knew this was what a real library was like. And this is just one row of books. One row of subjects."

Jason caressed the spine of a book. "I never get enough...." He caught himself. "Look. I don't want to be friends. I don't want people to even know I speak to you at work, okay?"

"Why? What have I done?" Maddy didn't like the idea of constantly being defensive with a co-worker.

"It's not only what you have done, but what you do every moment you breathe." Despite the horrible words, Jason's voice was quiet and matter-of-fact, like he had no intention of being cruel.

Maddy cocked her head, her heart beginning to feel the hurt of his words. She took a deep breath. "Okay. What have I done?"

"Look. I need to work. It's not the time or the place to discuss this."

"Where? When? At dinner? Do you eat in the dining room?"

"Don't you listen? I said I don't want people to see me speaking to you."

"Okay. Then how about if we talk in secret? In the back of the Pizza Den? On the street corner at night? Behind a bush? In the cedar grove?"

Jason didn't get her sarcasm, or pretended to ignore it. "Nowhere."

"You're not being fair!" Her anger flared. "I can't even find out what I've done wrong to see if I can make it right." Maddy looked deep into his eyes. She saw a solemn decision there. "Look," she said. "I know we had an accident. You weren't hurt. I wasn't hurt. We were both zipping along, a little too into our own speed. I ran a stop sign. You weren't really on your side of the street. Our angels were on duty because we totally missed each other. Otherwise I'd be dead, and you'd have to be mad on your own."

"It was your fault," Jason said, his eyes now becoming sharp with his anger. "I can't afford to fix my bike right. My parents can't afford to fix it right. And it's all your fault."

"It was an *accident*. No one meant for it to happen. I'm sorry your bike was damaged. But it's only a *thing*. It's only a bike." The minute the words left her mouth, Maddy saw Jason's anger rise.

"It's *only* a bike? I rebuilt that bike from the ground up. I put every nut and bolt on there myself. My friend in Minnesota did the paint job. That can never be replaced. That bike is my transportation. It's my baby."

By then, Maddy had had enough. She nodded as he spoke,

tight-lipped, ready to blast him with all she had. When he finished she smiled sweetly. "Oh. So a bike has more eternal value than I do." Now it was her turn to grab the book cart and turn away. She knew she should be sorry, but she wasn't. Not in the least.

"Look," Jason said hotly in her ear as he grabbed another book. "When you decide to really *be* a Christian instead of just pretending to be one, then maybe we can talk in public."

Maddy didn't even look up.

2

Maddy approached the circulation desk and leaned over the counter. "Alma," she said quietly.

Alma looked up from her work. "Yes, Maddy," she said brightly. "Will I see you tomorrow? Is everything going all right?"

Maddy wanted to tell her all about Jason and his bad attitude, but it seemed so juvenile to tattle. "I guess."

"I expect you to gain most of your information from Jason. I've assigned my junior and senior workers to a detailed task. You may ask them questions if Jason is not available, but I'd prefer that you didn't. The sooner they finish their project, the sooner they'll be back on the floor."

On the outside Maddy nodded, but on the inside she wanted to scream. Of all the people who worked in the library, why was she stuck with the one who totally disliked her? She'd watched Jason from a distance and had seen how he eagerly helped others. Never before had she seen someone so passionate about his work. Except her father. She wished Jason would let go of his anger and teach her what he knew. In a single day,

Maddy had discovered a hunger for knowledge she never knew existed. She wanted to know the library inside and out. And the one person who could help her satisfy that hunger hated her.

Maddy reluctantly opened the door to leave. Normally, she loved the nearly constant rain of Seattle. But now, she didn't want to leave the warm embrace of the library. She sighed and pulled her black, hooded wool cape over the three books she held in her arms.

Stepping into the rain, she moved at her usual quick pace. Maddy rarely walked slowly. In her mind, life needed to be taken in with great gusto. Without realizing it, she smiled as she imagined herself on a motorcycle—the rain and wind in her face.

"Gram would die," she said out loud. "And the school probably has some rule that says Maddy MacDonald is not allowed to own a motorcycle as long as she attends PCU. They have so many other stupid rules for me."

Following a strict set of rules was a new experience for Maddy. Gram had come to the school and negotiated with them to allow Maddy to attend, in spite of her low grades, meager finances, transcripts from over ten different high schools, *and* no extracurricular activities. Maddy had no idea what strings Gram pulled. She only knew her grandfather had played some big part in the school's formation. Gram had probably relied on Grandfather's reputation. As a result, the administration had allowed Maddy to come under a strict set of rules.

She had to live on campus, to allow Admin to keep a close eye on her grades and activities. They believed this would also limit distractions—such as commuting—that might keep her from her studies. She must be on a work-study program to pay for her way through school. If there was any drug use, or trouble with the law of any sort, Maddy would have no second chances. Lastly, her grade point average must be maintained at a 3.2 or better.

And, no doubt, no motorcycles allowed.

When she reached the dorm, she shook the excess rain off before opening the front door. Maddy loved this old building. She couldn't walk the wool-carpeted halls without imagining the voices of students from past years. She wondered what their lives were like. Did they think differently than she?

Her suite was on the second floor. She ran up the stairs two at a time, put her key in the lock, then moved through the quiet common living area and flung open the door to her room.

Sarah, as always, was at her desk studying. "So? How's the new job?" she asked without looking up.

Taking the books from their safe, dry, place, Maddy set them on her desk. "I've got a lot to learn."

Maddy liked her roommate, even though they couldn't be more different. Sarah came from a solid Christian family that lived in California. She had gone to a small Christian high school. Sarah never did anything wrong. Maddy figured she probably didn't even *think* of doing anything wrong. Her idea of being daring was sneaking out to TP someone's house without asking her parents. She'd done it once and felt so guilty, she never did it again.

Maddy, on the other hand, lived nowhere and everywhere. Her parents didn't think twice about God and encouraged

Maddy to experience whatever she wanted as long as it didn't hurt anyone. Therefore, Maddy had. She felt no guilt over anything she'd done until she made a daring decision to become a Christian.

Maddy smiled mischievously at her roommate. "I think I'm in love."

Sarah looked up from her books. "Yeah? Who is he? What's he look like? Do I know him?"

Maddy smiled. It seemed Sarah had only one thing on her mind. Find a suitable man, fall in love, and live happily ever after—after the picture-perfect wedding, of course.

Maddy chucked a dirty sock at her. "You goon! I'm in love with the library!"

Sarah cocked her head, her shoulder-length brown hair bouncing to one side. "In love with the library," she repeated in a flat tone.

Maddy flopped on her bed. She unlaced her boots, then popped them off expertly with each opposing foot. "Don't you think it's wonderful? Maybe I'm nuts. But there's something about that place—like it has its own life."

Sarah nodded once. "Uh, yeah." She stared at her book a moment, as if it might give her a clue to this mystery. "I'm sorry, Maddy. I don't get it. A library's a library. Lots of books. Why is this one different than any other library?"

"I don't know if it is different. I've never really been in a *library* before."

That got Sarah away from her books. "Excuse me? How can you be an American and not go to a library?"

Maddy rolled to one side and propped her head on her

hand. "I guess my parents didn't believe in them or something. When I was old enough to be able to read, we would be driving by a large building and I would see the word LIBRARY. A couple of times I asked if we could go in. Dad never would, though.

"'Why should we follow the foolish dreams of old men?' he said once. 'It will only lock us in and make us stay.' Or something like that."

"What in the world does that mean?" Sarah looked as confused as Maddy had always felt when her dad said something mysterious.

Maddy pulled back her red hair with her long fingers. "I don't know. He wouldn't say anything more than that."

"And you never snuck off to one?" Sarah asked, tapping her pencil on the desk. "You snuck off and did everything else."

Maddy laughed. "Not *everything* else. I snuck off to parties and to go places with friends. Somehow sneaking off to a library wasn't at the top of my list."

Sarah looked at her with narrowed eyes. "I don't believe you never went to any library in your entire life."

"Actually, the only libraries I went to were the ones in the elementary schools and in some of the high schools I went to. Small rooms. A few books on the walls. Nothing terribly interesting. Certainly nothing like *this*."

Maddy dropped back on the bed and immediately became lost in a daydream in which she was back in the ancient building, wandering up and down the aisles, skimming book titles —amazed at the wealth of information offered there.

"We're invited to some rally," Sarah interrupted.

Coming out of her reverie, Maddy focused on Sarah, but didn't answer.

"Some church is putting it on. A bigger one than Capitol Community Center. Sunday night. I really want to go, but I'm not used to big groups of people. Will you come?"

"Do you want me? Or will anybody do?" Maddy teased.

Sarah chucked the dirty sock back at Maddy. "I want *you* to come. You're more comfortable with new people than I am. Maybe some of you will rub off on me."

"Just so long as you don't rub off on me." Maddy made a face.

"I do adore you roomie," Sarah said dryly. "You are always so affirming."

Maddy playfully threw her a saccharine smile. "Thank you. I try."

That night, after spending two hours studying cells for Biology, Maddy took the top book off her library stack and snuggled into bed. Her first selection was the story of a real person.

While at the library, she had been amazed to see how many books were about people. Not even about subjects. Just people's life stories. How they lived. How they grew up. How they fit in—or didn't fit in—to the world. After Maddy finished her work, she had gone back to that section. To narrow her choices, she ignored all the books about famous people. History bored her, so she didn't want to read about any historical figures. Politics was far worse than history, so she skipped those. And then, she found a gem—*A Girl and Five Brave Horses*.

Until now, Maddy had avoided reading like she'd avoided all school work. She only read what was absolutely necessary to pass her classes. Even then, she fudged reading the required novels, never opening them unless she actually happened to stay in that town long enough for the report to actually be due. She had a tried–and–true method for gaining enough of the gist of the story by reading the first and last chapters, and a sentence or two of every chapter in between. She always got passing grades on the few reports she had to do. But she never had to do many of them. New teachers always felt sorry for her and generally gave her an alternate assignment to do that was far easier than going back and reading the whole book the class had been studying for a month or more.

Maddy was really surprised when Sarah complained in a groggy voice, "Maddy, when are you going to turn off that light? It's after one o'clock."

Forty pages had gone by, and Maddy hadn't even noticed. Forty pages of a fascinating life much like her own. A fragmented family, but without the malls.

Maddy switched off the light. That night, she dreamed that she was the main character in her book and had run away to join a circus.

3

The next morning, the phone rang in the suite's living room. Without answering it, Sarah called out, "That'll be your grandmother, Maddy."

Maddy reluctantly put down her book and glanced at the clock. Right on time. Gram called every Saturday at eleven. She moved to the common room and answered the phone. "Hi, Gram."

"How did you know it was me? It could have been anyone. Maybe your father," Gram said, sounding indignant that the granddaughter she hardly knew had her so well pegged.

"Gram! Think again. My father, call? Your son?"

As soon as she heard her grandmother's deep sigh, Maddy knew she shouldn't have said it. She quickly changed the subject. "Gram, I finally got a job in the work-study program!"

"Well, I'm glad. Where do you work?"

"The library."

Maddy heard her grandmother catch her breath. "The library?"

"Yes. And I love it. I feel something very different when I walk in there."

"And well you should, dear." Gram's voice seemed to smile over the line. "Grandfather would be pleased."

Maddy pondered that a second, but it didn't compute. She figured it was just another one of the odd things Gram popped up with all the time.

"I'm doing okay, Gram."

"The office says you're doing fine so far, but they wish your grades were higher."

"They called again?"

"They call every Friday."

"This is worse than being in high school. No one monitored me there. Why can't they leave me alone?"

"There's more at stake here, dear. They've taken a financial risk with you. They've made allowances to let you enroll in spite of your poor school records. They've only let you attend because of your grandfather's reputation and my promise that I will make sure you toe the line."

"I know." Maddy twisted a strand of hair around her finger. "I am studying hard, Gram. I really am." She wanted to make her grandmother proud. She didn't know why. Maybe she hoped to connect with one family member in her lifetime.

"I'm worried about you trying to work two jobs and study. That's an awful lot to put on a young girl."

Maddy wanted to protest—at the very least about being a young girl. But she knew her Gram just used words that came to her. She didn't intend to hurt. Still, the part about working too hard and having to study—Maddy, too, was worried about trying to juggle it all. Her heavy study schedule scared her to death. She'd never had anyone care before about whether she got As or Fs. She'd never even been taught how to study. These classes were far more difficult than anything she'd done in the countless high schools she'd attended. And she had to work two jobs on top of it.

"Maddy? Do you think you can do it?"

"I'm trying, Gram."

"If you need to come here on the weekends to study properly, you do that. I don't want all the temptations of parties and such to distract you from what is most important."

The thought of staying with the woman she hardly knew didn't appeal to Maddy. She was glad she had a legitimate excuse. "I can't stay with you, Gram. I have to work at Starbucks on the weekends. It's too far for me to go from your house to work."

"I know," Gram said, her voice held a trace of longing. "I'll let you know if I hear from your parents."

"I guess that means I won't hear from you until next Saturday," Maddy said bluntly.

After a deep breath, Gram spoke in her cheery voice. "Yes, you certainly will. And very soon we're going to have Thanksgiving together. Maddy, there's a program at the university that I have participated in every year." She paused a moment. "I wanted to find out what you would think about me becoming involved again this year."

"Why would it matter what I think, Gram?"

"Because it involves you," Gram stated.

Maddy was terribly confused now. "How could something you have participated in every year involve me?"

"Every year, there are kids at the university who have

nowhere to go over Thanksgiving vacation. Those of us in and around Seattle who are associated with the university are often asked if we might volunteer to have a student or two for the weekend. I have always had two students. Since you are here this year, I do not want to have any if it would upset you…or if you planned on having a nice dinner alone—just the two of us."

Maddy relaxed on the floor, dropping her head back to rest on the sofa. "Gram," she said to the ceiling, "I think it would be wonderful to have a stray or two over for the weekend." *Then I'll be sure to have someone to talk to.* "I had no idea you did stuff like that."

"A stray? Maddy, dear, I hope you don't say that in front of the person." Gram sounded offended.

"Well, we hope the people have a sense of humor, or maybe they shouldn't come!" Maddy teased.

"Maddy!"

"Just kidding, Gram."

As they wound up the conversation, Maddy pictured her grandmother—tall, stocky, big-boned—not like the stereotypical soft, plump sort of grandmother. Gram did have the standard, gray curly hair, with only hints of the red it must have been years before. She also had the eyeglasses and the odd, out-of-date clothes. Maddy had only been with Gram once in her entire life—when she had visited her for two weeks before school began.

For some reason unknown to her, Maddy's father had stopped speaking to his parents sometime before she was born. It took a full year of Maddy begging them to let her to go to a university before they finally relented and allowed her to contact her grandmother in Seattle. They gave one strict condition —that Maddy make all the arrangements herself. They did not want to speak to Gram.

"Thanks again for taking *me* in," Maddy said suddenly, still amazed that Gram would even speak to her after all the years of silence. She hoped that one day they would really talk.

"You're welcome," Gram said, making it sound more like she'd done her duty.

An awkward silence hung between them before they both said their good-byes.

As she hung up, Maddy wondered who God would put in Gram's house for Thanksgiving. Whoever it was, the distraction would certainly take her mind off the tangible awkwardness between her and Gram.

Sarah stuck her head out the bedroom door. "Going to lunch?"

"In a minute." Outside the bedroom window, the sky was the usual dreary gray. Maddy pulled a tight black sweater over her head, tugging it to just above her belly button. Then she yanked off her boxers and replaced them with an Indian-patterned skirt. Nineteen silver bracelets and one long earring completed the outfit. She bent over, brushed her red hair quickly, then flipped it all back in one quick motion. "Ready."

So much had changed since she first walked into the dorm room in September! Maddy had to smile at the memory of Sarah's horrified face when she first laid eyes on her. The girl had clearly thought she'd gotten stuck with the roommate horror of the century. It took Sarah some time to realize that Maddy's faith was true and that although her clothes were offbeat, they fit

Maddy's personality. Now the girls' friendship was growing.

Maddy really liked Sarah's stability and level-headed approach to most of life. In turn, Sarah was drawn to Maddy's wild ideas, new faith, and experience of being brought up with unlimited freedom.

In the cafeteria, Sarah and Maddy took their lunch trays to the salad bar. Maddy loaded up on lettuce, radishes, red onion, and lots of ranch dressing. Sarah dabbled in the pasta, Jell-o, and sunflower seeds. Both girls got glasses of punch before moving toward the tables. "Do you care where we sit?" Sarah asked over her shoulder.

Maddy shook her head. "Lead on." Paying no attention to where Sarah walked, Maddy sucked punch through a straw while she walked. She plunked her tray next to Sarah and sat. Looking up, she caught Jason's startled look from the opposite side of the table. His eyes narrowed. Grabbing his tray, he stood up, quietly turned around, and sat at the next table with his back to Maddy.

"Hey, Maddy—you didn't tell me you had a secret admirer." Sarah jabbed a pasta spiral and popped it into her mouth.

"Lucky me." Once again, Jason had managed to slice Maddy wide open. She focused on her salad and pretended it didn't matter. What she really wanted to do was to blast him in front of everybody. But her new life in God made her feel she should back off and give the whole situation time. *Please,* she wanted to say to God. *Let me at him.*

The three other guys at the table stared at Jason's back, then at Maddy. "What's with him?" a clean-cut blond asked.

"I'm his favorite person in the whole world," Maddy

answered. She put on a fake smile.

"I can see that," the guy with the dark complexion and round, dark eyes agreed, his sarcasm obvious. He wore a maroon sweatshirt with a small PCU logo. "What made you the favorite person?" He tilted his head to take a bite from a bulging taco.

"I think it's a secret. Ask him and then let me know. He won't tell me." Maddy ate, trying not to let on that the whole thing disturbed her. She didn't often have people hate her. But when they did, there was usually a good reason for it.

"Hey, Jason. What's your problem with Irish, here?" the third guy called out. He wore a Seattle Seahawks sport cap backward. Maddy couldn't tell for sure what color his hair was.

Jason didn't answer. He continued to shovel away his lunch as fast as he could.

"She's too pretty to hate." Seattle Seahawks smiled at her. Maddy accepted the compliment with a dip of her head.

His comment got a reaction. Jason turned slowly and stared at his friend.

"We're getting somewhere," the blond stated to his friends, flashing them the thumbs-up sign.

"Do you hate her because she's pretty?" PCU sweatshirt asked.

Jason kept eating.

"Look, guys. I was just kidding," Maddy said. "I really don't know why he hates me. But why don't you leave him alone?" She dragged one finger across her neck in a cutting motion, indicating that she wanted them to stop the interrogation.

The three looked at each other and shrugged. Jason got up and left.

Sarah tried to balance sunflower seeds on her fork. "Really, Maddy, do you know what his problem is?"

Maddy thought a moment, then noticed the eager faces across from her. "I suppose it's because of the motorcycle accident."

"Did you see it?" Seahawks asked. "Man, he was ticked about that."

Maddy sighed. "I was on a bicycle."

"Oh, the Wicked Witch!" PCU sweatshirt exclaimed.

"You're the chick from the "Wizard of Oz" song." Seahawks began to hum a little tune, then said in a creaky voice, "'I'll get you, my pretty, and your little dog, too!'"

Maddy scrunched up her face, listening. "Jason has hummed that a couple of times in the library."

Sarah's eyes grew wide. "The library! He works with you, doesn't he? No wonder you looked so stressed when you came back yesterday."

"Did you knock over his bike there, too?" the blond guy asked.

"I didn't *knock* over his bike. I was riding my bicycle, he was riding his motorcycle, I blew a stop sign, he was on the wrong side of the street. It was an *accident.*"

"Not the way he tells it."

The three guys stared at her as if she was the personification of something evil.

Maddy felt frustrated. Didn't anyone know the meaning of *accident?*

Sarah put her fork down. She scanned the faces in front of her, then turned to Maddy. "This is real serious, isn't it?"

One of the three wise men shook his head. "I sure wouldn't want to be on Jason's bad side. He's one of those complicated types. Pretty serious about life. He approaches all people, his friends, his future, his studies and his work with a judgemental eye. Always searching for the truth, he says."

Seahawks downed one of three glasses of milk in a single gulp, wiped his mouth with the back of his sleeve, then added, "Jason's Bible Man."

Sarah leaned forward. "So? What does that mean?"

PCU leaned forward as if ready to disclose a secret. "What my atheist friend here means is that Jason spends a lot of time studying his Bible, searching for what God demands of his followers."

Blondie piped up. "Jason wants everyone else to live by God's rules too."

Maddy's gaze took on her target. "But I'm obeying God's rules. I thought the Bible was more about grace than judgment."

The three guys laughed, as though at an inside joke.

Maddy nodded. "Now I know the problem."

Sarah's head swiveled toward her. "What?"

"Look at me, Sarah."

Sarah looked into her eyes. "Yeah."

Maddy stood up. "No. *Look* at me." She held out her arms. She blushed, but knew she needed to make a point.

The guys took the invitation seriously. They all nodded in appreciation. Sarah also looked, but her face registered total confusion. She looked at the guys and noticed their admiration. She looked back at Maddy. "I still don't get it."

Maddy eagerly sat back in her chair. "Do you guys get it? What would Jason see when he looks at me?"

"Either a mission field or target practice," PCU offered.

"Bingo," Maddy said. "He knows I'm a Christian. That leaves target practice."

Sarah slowly shook her head. "I still don't get it."

Maddy looked dead into Sarah's eyes. "Sarah. I dress—well, I dress differently than a lot of people."

Sarah nodded, still not understanding.

Maddy sagged a little, looking up at the loft over the dining area while she thought. "Okay. I dress different than *most* people. And when you look at me, what do you think?"

"That I'd like to borrow some of your clothes."

The guys all laughed.

"Sarah," Maddy said. "Jason thinks clothes like these aren't for Christians. He's told me as much."

"What's wrong with a skirt, sweater, and some jewelry?"

"I agree. But I guess Jason doesn't."

Seahawks had finished his chocolate cake and downed the last glass of milk. "Bible Man has a strict dress and behavior code. Beware!"

Sarah stared at Maddy. "What are you going to do?"

"Nothing." Maddy turned to the table guests. "Thanks for clearing up the mystery. I thought it was the accident all along." Standing, she picked up her tray and bused it at the dining room window. Sarah followed close behind. "Really, Maddy. You should think of something to do."

Maddy looked at her watch. "I have thought of something to do. I'm going to go to work."

4

The same short, nervous, balding man who owned the Starbucks on Pill Hill also owned The Cup & Chaucer, a cozy, scholarly coffee house on Capitol Hill near the university. Maddy had never been there. Life had been a whirlwind ever since she set foot in Seattle less than four months before. Sightseeing had to wait.

Joe Plimco—the short, nervous, balding owner—had hired Maddy to work at Starbucks in early October, and had trained her in specialty coffee finesse and etiquette. Maddy learned quickly. Her favorite part of the job was the customers. She loved making them smile—especially if they were having a bad day. She discovered that often, all she needed to do was smile first. Her friendliness and joy in serving seemed to brighten their day.

When Maddy arrived at work, Joe met her at the door. "Sorry I'm late, Joe," she said.

Looking at his watch, Joe shook his head. "Only two minutes, Maddy. You're getting better." He put his hand in the middle of her back and directed her toward a table in the corner. "I want you to sit here. Don't get too comfortable. We're making a change."

Maddy sat, dropping her soft cloth purse to the floor. She chewed on the inside of her cheek, watching everything going on around her. A new girl was behind the counter, trying hard to catch on to all the nuances of achieving the right mix of Italian coffee and steaming milk for what was probably her first cappuccino. Maddy felt sorry for her—but also was afraid this was a sign that she had been replaced. Her heart sank. She really needed this second job to help pay for school. Even worse, if she was let go, the Admin Committee might feel even more wary about her presence in their school.

Joe trotted over and leaned on the back of a chair.

"You've decided I shouldn't work here any more, haven't you, Joe?" Maddy asked, wanting to get it over with as soon as possible.

Joe grinned. "I always knew you were smarter than most. You've got it."

Maddy sighed and picked up her purse. "Okay. Thanks for the chance, Joe. I appreciate it."

"Where're you goin'?" Joe asked, his bushy brows furrowed together in confusion.

"Back to school," Maddy said, her voice flat as she tried to hold back her tears.

"I didn't tell you to leave," Joe said.

"But you said my job here was over." Maddy felt confused.

"Sure did. But I ain't lettin' you outta my sight." Joe winked at her. "I'm takin' you to my other store."

"Where's that?"

"Closer to the university. That way you can mingle with your own sort, and maybe not be late all the time. Come on." Joe moved quickly, not waiting to see if Maddy followed.

Once outside, Joe threw Maddy's bike into the trunk of his rattletrap Impala. He then drove her to a small coffee shop just three blocks from campus. The building had huge storefront windows with thick, medieval-style letters painted in forest green and outlined in gold, THE CUP & CHAUCER.

Joe pushed open the door to the tinkle of a bell. Maddy followed close behind. She put her hand to her chest, her heart fluttering for the second time in two days. It took a moment for her eyes to adjust to the subdued light—but her nose had alerted her first. That new scent she had experienced at the library also filled the air here. Mixed with the smell of coffee, it was the most divine fragrance on earth.

When her eyes adjusted, Maddy could see the books. Hundreds of them. Maybe thousands. Old volumes lined the walls, floor to ceiling. She dropped her purse right where she stood and moved silently across the room. Her hands brushed the bindings, her eyes scanned the titles.

"You like books?" Joe asked.

"Hmmm. A new interest," Maddy muttered.

"You can dust them then," he said with a chuckle.

"It's a deal. I'd love to," Maddy said, without taking her eyes off the shelves.

Joe wobbled his head, talking to the person behind the coffee bar. "Hey. And I was just joking."

"Take her up on it," said the tall lumberjack behind the counter.

"These here are my pride and joy," Joe said, leading Maddy to a row of glass cases. "They're all fourteenth century to eighteenth century reproductions of Chaucer's works."

"Wow," Maddy said, peering in at a copy of *The Canterbury Tales*. It was open to an elaborately illustrated page.

"I'm kinda partial to Chaucer," Joe added. "Studied him at school years ago. Got caught up in the coffee thing, though. Never could decide which I loved more. Coffee or books."

He wandered to the bar while Maddy stared at the ancient texts. "Maddy. Come over here. Wantcha to meet Brad. He's the other coffee kook here."

Maddy left the books and moved across the room. She reached across the bar and shook Brad's wide, thick hand with a firm grip. "Nice to meet you."

Brad bowed a little and did a half-dance shuffle backwards.

After Joe left, Maddy wandered around the store, trying to get her bearings. The room was littered with mismatched sofas and overstuffed chairs, probably bought at estate sales. A coffee table had been positioned in front of each group of seats. Old, converted gas lamps hung from the ceiling. At the rear of the remodeled tavern sat a small platform, painted forest green. Behind the platform a flyer had been stuck on a bookshelf, its top edge pinned underneath some books, then bent down so people could read about the next event—OPEN POETRY READING, SATURDAY 8:30 P.M.

"Anybody show up to these things?" Maddy called to Brad.

"Depends. Tonight we'll have some local wannabes. Later in the school year, as more and more students come, the locals will get disgusted and drop out."

Maddy moved toward the front of the tavern to the bar. She let her hand move along the solid wood. "This bar is beautiful."

"All polished mahogany. Brass accents. A pain to keep clean, but really a fine piece of work."

"Desserts?" Maddy asked, lifting a glass dome off a silver pedestal.

"Brownies, some weird cake, Bernie's Bagels. We could use something better. But we live with what we've got."

Maddy wandered over to a tall, round table with stools surrounding it. Sitting on it were several laptop computers. A brass sign had usage prices engraved in it. "This is great."

Brad nodded. "There's a few more scattered about. Most everyone uses them for e-mail or schoolwork."

Maddy came back to the bar. Her eye caught an old-fashioned cash register off to one side. "Do you use that?"

"Not in the mornings. I've got some students who'll man those during the busy hours. Your job is to stick with the coffee, books, and people-pleasing."

"I can do that," Maddy said brightly. She wondered which place was going to be more fun—The Cup & Chaucer or the library.

Just then, a subtle bell rang as the door opened. A group of students moved in at once. Without thinking twice, Maddy slipped behind the counter and began to serve up coffee—straights and fancies.

At times that afternoon, Maddy felt like she had never made a cup of coffee before. The equipment at The Cup & Chaucer was different enough that she felt she had to learn all over again. She learned fast, but not fast enough for her own comfort. The day moved quickly into evening. When the poetry reading began, Maddy moved about the tavern like a cocktail waitress, gliding between the tables, cleaning up glasses, and offering refills.

Brad nodded his approval. "I see why Joe brought you down here. I didn't think I really needed much help. But you've helped us bring in more money than we've ever brought in on a reading night. Mostly they get one cup and get too caught up in the poetry to come back to the bar for more. Good job."

Maddy smiled. She didn't get many pats on the back. She had always worked hard at her jobs and the good places had recognized and praised her. The horrible ones had taken advantage or criticized her even when she did what they'd asked.

Despite Brad's praise, the evening was long. And it wasn't until after midnight that Maddy fell into bed, exhausted.

Sunday morning Maddy woke, wondering if she should go to church. She loved worshipping. She loved learning more and more about this God she had met nine months before. What she didn't like were the stares and glares from the well-dressed church women and surreptitious glances from their husbands, or their outright disdain.

Sarah's face appeared two inches from Maddy's. "You're coming, aren't you?"

Maddy rolled to her back so Sarah wouldn't keel over and die from her morning breath. "I don't know, Sarah. Where is it we're going tonight?"

"To The Club Gathering."

Maddy thought a minute. "I'll wait and get my church there. I have to study, then work this afternoon." Maddy turned to look at Sarah, who turned her mouth into a frown.

"You aren't helping yourself any," Sarah said, adjusting her sweater.

"What's that supposed to mean?"

"If you want Jason to like you, you have to at least go to church."

"In this world there are millions of Jasons. They will never understand someone like me. I can go to church every day and night of the week. But until I start living according to his rules, I still won't be acceptable. So why bother trying?"

"Fine. Just don't say I didn't warn you."

Sarah left, and Maddy rolled out of bed. After a short, water-conserving shower, she dressed and went for a walk. The Cup & Chaucer wouldn't be open yet. Nor would most anything else. She meandered through the streets until she came across a large church where people spilled onto the street. More streamed through the doors. Maddy followed them.

Without looking to see if anyone noticed her, she moved toward the sanctuary. A man wearing a cowboy shirt and hat smiled and handed her a program. "Good morning," he said, without even glancing at the rest of her. Maddy returned the smile.

She slipped into the rear pew, hoping to survive there unno-ticed. As the church filled, Mr. Cowboy Hat walked in and out of the sanctuary several times, greeting people and directing them. On one of his trips he stopped. "I'd like you to meet my wife. Would you mind?"

Maddy didn't know what to say. Normally she would have been thrilled to meet anyone new. Today she preferred to be alone. But she didn't want to hurt his feelings. Besides, she really had no clue how to get out of it truthfully and gracefully. "Okay," she said hesitantly.

Maddy followed him toward the front of the church. It wasn't until they reached the third row, where she met Mrs. Wilson—Mrs. Cowboy Hat—that Maddy realized there was something different about this church. When she went to church with Sarah, conversations stopped and people stared at Maddy. Here, not a single one stopped. Mrs. Wilson didn't give her a strange look. Only a welcoming smile.

"College student?" she asked, as Maddy sat next to her.

Maddy nodded. "I'm a freshman at Pacific Cascades University."

Mrs. Wilson pulled back, an admiring look in her face. "Gorgeous campus. Good school. You must be smart."

Maddy blushed. "I don't know about that." The choir filed in. Maddy was relieved that the service was about to begin so she wouldn't have to talk about school any more.

Mrs. Wilson patted her knee then pointed at a portly man with gray hair. "That one's our pastor," she said, then turned her attention to the front.

Mr. Wilson slipped in beside his wife after the worship service began. He held his hat in his hands and sang exuberantly.

After the service, Mrs. Wilson rolled her eyes and looked at her husband. "Bill, I don't know why we didn't tell Maddy about the college class. She would have had a much better time there rather than sitting with us old fogies." She turned to

Maddy. "I read in the bulletin that the college class is having some sort of party tonight. I guess Ron wants all the freshmen from the universities around here to get together and meet the older students. So the Christians can at least recognize one another on campus. Maybe you could come."

Maddy couldn't believe it. "That's here? My roommate and I plan to come."

"Good. I know there's lots of kids—I'm sorry, students—who come. So it ought to be lots of fun."

Maddy thanked them, declined their invitation to lunch, and left the church. Walking with her head high this time, she was able to return many friendly hellos.

Maddy didn't have much time to get ready between work at The Cup & Chaucer and the party. She found Sarah pacing the living room, talking to herself. "I'll wear my hair up. No, it's too short. It looks stupid. I'll French braid it. No. But what if my hair doesn't go with my clothes? I don't know how to do this. Oh, Maddy! There you are. You've got to help me!"

Maddy took Sarah's hand and dragged her into their room. Together, they stood in front of Maddy's closet. "What do you want to wear?"

"I love your deep red sweater."

Maddy cocked her head, picturing the cropped piece of clothing. "Have you ever worn anything that has shown one square inch of your skin?"

Sarah shook her head.

"Can you handle it?"

"What's there to handle? I'll be fine. Can I wear it?" Her words said she was okay with it, but her cheeks grew a little flushed.

Maddy paused a moment. She didn't mind loaning her things. But she wasn't sure Sarah would really feel comfortable. "What would you wear with it?"

"You choose."

In the face of Sarah's excitement, Maddy could not turn her down. She knew Sarah would look dynamite in a pair of black leggings, the red sweater, and big silver earrings, with her hair held up in a black butterfly clip. She also pictured adding a solid silver choker, black flats, and make-up. Sarah refused the choker, not wanting to go overboard.

"I'm not sure I like this," Sarah said, turning in front of the mirror. "It's...."

"That's okay," Maddy said, smiling. She rifled through Sarah's clothes. "Here, wear this instead." She handed Sarah a bulky green sweater that was soft and pretty. "The leggings are enough for you to get used to in one night."

In minutes the transformation left them both staring in the mirror.

"I'm jealous," Maddy finally whispered.

"Whoa." Sarah said. She kept turning from side to side, staring at herself.

Maddy thrashed through her clothes, trying to figure out something to wear. She didn't want to look like she was competing with Sarah, so she'd have to choose something really different. She settled on skin-tight cream pants with a short, loose, sky-blue angora sweater. She messed up her hair, then put on light lipstick and liner.

"We'll knock 'em dead." Sarah said, throwing her purse over her shoulder.

"Yes, we will," Maddy said with what she hoped was a bright smile. "Yes, we will."

5

"Aren't you nervous, Maddy?" Sarah asked as they walked through the drizzle.

Maddy shook her head. "I love meeting new people. My father always said meeting new people was an adventure in the future. And that if you're real lucky, you'll also have a glimpse into the past."

"What did he mean by that?"

Maddy frowned. "You never know when you're going to meet someone who will change your life, I guess."

"Is that why he likes his job so much?"

Maddy shrugged. "I suppose. He also says he's looking for the one face he's missing in life."

"And who would that be?" Sarah tilted her head, looking at Maddy as they walked.

"I don't know," Maddy sighed. "He never would tell me. He just said he'd let me know when he found it. Of course he never did, so the mystery still lives."

Sarah scrunched her face. "Parents can be so weird."

Maddy smiled. From what she'd heard, Sarah's parents were about as normal as they came.

The large upstairs room at the church was overflowing with students. Some sat in chairs that were lined up in rows. Others mingled, talking with old friends and making new ones. Sarah grabbed Maddy's arm. "Wait. I don't know about this."

Maddy looked at Sarah in surprise. Basically strong Sarah changed drastically in crowds of people she didn't know. "It's okay," Maddy reassured her. "People are nice most of the time. If not, you just go to the next group."

Sarah's grip tightened. "Isn't your heart racing?"

Maddy shook her head. "Nope. This is fun for me."

"I'm terrified." Sarah looked it. Her eyes were wide, her face pale.

Maddy thought a moment. It was hard for her to imagine being terrified of meeting people. Sometimes she wasn't in the mood for it, but she never felt scared. She chewed her lip. "Look, Sarah. I'm sorry I'm clueless as to how you feel. You can go sit down if you'd like that better."

Sarah gulped and let go of Maddy's arm. She held her chin up. "Let's go. Maybe I'll learn something."

Maddy led Sarah to the middle of the most crowded part of the room. "Hi, I'm Maddy MacDonald," she said to a mixed group. "We don't know a soul, and thought you looked least likely to throw us out of the room." Many faces turned toward them. Some looked startled as they noticed Maddy's navel ring. Others noticed, but took it in stride.

"Hi, Maddy, I'm Kick." A good-looking, long-haired guy with a well-trimmed goatee smiled and stuck out his hand to her. "My real name's Robert, but it doesn't go with the personal-ity."

"And Kick does?" Maddy asked, teasing.

"Of course! And it's certainly better than Robert—agreed?" He smiled again.

Maddy laughed. "Sure." Kick wore patched, but clean jeans. His T-shirt was mostly hidden by a faded leather vest. After he shook hands with Sarah, he deftly pulled his dark hair back into a low ponytail.

At Maddy's insistence, the others in the group introduced themselves. She asked each of them where they were from and which school they went to. Most were from PCU, and surpris-ingly, many were upperclassmen.

Sarah kept quiet, watching Maddy's every move. She only made a noise when saying a quick "Hi," to those introduced to her.

"So, what's going on tonight?" Maddy asked the group.

"A Foot Rally."

"What's that?"

"We break up into groups of ten. Then we're given an ancient Polaroid camera and a list of crazy things to do," a girl told her.

"We take pictures to prove we've done all the things on the list," a skinny little guy added. "First team back wins."

"How do they break us up into teams?"

"We can choose," the skinny guy said. "With you two, we'd be ten. Want to join us?"

Maddy glanced at Sarah to get her okay. Sarah gave a slight nod. "Looks like you've got your ten."

In her mind, Maddy went around the group several times,

repeating their names over and over. She loved her own name and knew it was important that she remember everyone else's.

Kick sneaked up behind Maddy and put his hands on her shoulders. "Looks like a bunch of sheep in this room," he whispered in her ear.

"Baaaa," Maddy answered.

"Not you." He peered around at her face, then whispered again. "*You* are a breath of fresh air."

Maddy smiled. "You mean I'm different." She experienced a feeling of warmth at the special attention he paid to her.

Kick nodded wholeheartedly. "You have a space of your own."

He moved away, sauntering over to the punch table. Maddy watched him go. He, too, was obviously his own person. She liked him immediately.

"You sure you want us on your team?" Maddy asked the others.

When they all agreed, Maddy said, "Okay. Then save me a place. I want to go meet some other people."

Maddy made the rounds of the room, trying to meet and have a brief conversation with as many people as she could. Sarah followed along behind, saying her shy hello whenever she had to speak. Maddy felt like there was an invisible strand of rope tying them together. Sarah never got more than three feet away, always hovering a little to Maddy's right. Maddy felt sorry for Sarah, the ultimate introvert and wallflower when it came to social situations. She wished she could help her roommate come out of her shell, but wasn't sure how. She figured Sarah could learn best by observing.

Sarah kept tugging at her sweater, as if feeling self-conscious about her slim-fitting pants. Over in the corner, a group huddled in the shadows. "I'm going to get those shy people to come out and join the rest of us," Maddy announced.

"I wish you wouldn't," Sarah said. "I'm afraid they'll look at us like we're strange."

"Maybe they will, but if you want to learn how to meet people, you have to learn to meet everyone, Sarah."

"Okay." Sarah reluctantly followed Maddy.

Maddy strode up to the group, her voice loud and friendly. "Okay, folks, hide and seek is over. We found you, now you're It."

Several pairs of surprised eyes gazed up at her and a couple of people smiled shyly in response. Maddy offered her hand to a girl dressed in black slacks, flowered blouse, and knit vest.

"Hi, I'm Laura," the girl said, then seemed to go blank.

"I can't believe it!" a voice whispered in Maddy's ear.

Turning, Maddy saw glowering eyes. "I'm just trying to be friendly," she said defensively.

Jason crossed his arms. "I'm not sure you belong here."

Maddy tried to push her frustration aside. "I thought this was an event open to anyone interested in meeting new people."

Jason sighed and dropped his arms. "Do you really want to meet these kinds of people? Wouldn't you be more at home at a different kind of party?" He sounded like he really believed it.

Maddy shook her head in disbelief. "Why are you so intent on hurting me?"

Jason's face changed. He dropped his gaze to the floor. He didn't answer at first. "Look, I'm not trying to hurt you. I just feel this group has a sense of solidarity and commitment to something you wouldn't be interested in."

Maddy shook her head in disgust. "Nice to know everyone is no longer welcome into the Kingdom."

"Jesus never welcomed the Pharisees."

Maddy struggled to remember who the Pharisees were.

Sarah tugged on Maddy's sleeve. "Come on, Maddy. Let's get out of here."

Maddy was about to disagree. But her roommate looked pale and shaken. "Okay," she said softly. "We'll go where people welcome us."

Jason said nothing more, but Maddy could feel his gaze bore into her back. It gave her a ticklish feeling and she shivered. She hoped he hadn't noticed.

Back in their saved seats, Maddy tried to forget Jason's hurtful words. She whispered a quick prayer. "God. What's wrong with Jason? Or is there something wrong with me? What can I do to make things better?"

The leader interrupted Maddy's quiet prayer with instructions for the rally. Maddy's team got an early start, since they already had chosen their ten players. Their first stop was a laundromat where one person had to be inside the dryer for the picture. Tiny Tim popped inside without being asked.

Next, they had to shove everyone into a phone booth. At the grocery store, they all had to be taking a bite of the same cookie. There, they chipped in to buy rolls of toilet paper to wrap one person up on the corner of Aloha and 15th Ave. Tiny Tim again volunteered to be the victim.

Dumb stuff, Maddy surmised, but a lot of crazy fun. And

they quickly learned each other's personalities. They got turned around and ran the wrong way down Pill Hill after taking their picture in front of one of the seven hospitals. That wrong turn cost them the win, but they didn't care. Breathless, they stormed the church, arriving second. They posted their photos on a bulletin board underneath the winning team's. Slurping hot coffee and cocoa, they snagged handfuls of chocolate chip cookies.

Kick grabbed Maddy's wrist. "Come on. Let's sit near the board. We can check out the pics as they come in."

"Umm!" Maddy said, her mouth full of cookie. "Sarah. Come on."

At the board, Kick sat, pulling Maddy into his lap.

"Yes, Santa. I've been a good girl," she said in a tiny voice. She felt awkward sitting there, but didn't want Kick to know that. "I want a Barbie doll and a Ken to play with." She batted her eyes heavily, then slipped off his knee.

Sarah watched, her eyes missing nothing.

As the pictures went up, Kick had something to say about them all. "Look at Fatty Patty here, good thing they didn't try to put her in the dryer." Then, "Oh, I thought this was a flag pole. It's some guy on their team."

Each dig was said with a jovial spirit and in some sort of funny voice, so Maddy couldn't help but laugh. Sarah smiled nervously, as if she felt she was eavesdropping.

After coupons for a free hamburger from Johnny Rockets were given to the winning team members, Kick turned to Maddy and Sarah.

"Mind if I walk you ladies home this evening?"

"How nice!" Maddy said, glancing at Sarah, wondering what she thought.

"Okay," Sarah said.

"Allow me." Kick tucked one hand in each elbow and maneuvered the girls through the crowd. He had them laughing in no time. And in no time they were back at the dorm.

"Thank you so very much," Maddy said.

"Indeed, my pleasure," Kick said in a mock gentleman's voice. He kissed the top of both girls' heads and waved goodbye.

Sarah moved through the hall, shuffling her feet across the rose carpet. She had a half-smile on her face, her eyes glazed over.

Maddy waved her hand in front of her. "Yoo-hoo. Anyone home?"

"He kissed me."

"On top of the head, yeah."

A big smile spread across Sarah's face. She sighed. "Yeah." She tenderly touched the spot on the top of her head.

Maddy contemplated whether to pop Sarah's bubble or not. She decided since this must be Sarah's first kiss, she should let it stay bright and shiny. She shook her head and put the key in their door. "We're home, Cinderella."

For the next hour, Sarah talked of nothing but Kick. "He's so cute, Maddy. Don't you think so? Do you think he really likes us? He is so funny. I couldn't stop laughing."

"Sarah. You didn't say a word all night," Maddy said, confused. "You never once laughed out loud."

"No. But I was howling on the inside. I was too embarrassed

to laugh out loud. What if he thinks I laugh strange? What if I say something stupid? What if I come across as a complete idiot?"

"So what?"

Sarah stopped twirling her flannel nightgown ribbon around her finger. Her head popped up, her eyes wide.

"So what if he thinks you laugh strange?" Maddy insisted. "Be yourself. If a guy can't like you for who you are, just like you are, then forget it."

"But what if he doesn't like me?"

"Sarah. God made you just the way you are for a reason. Don't ever try to be someone you aren't. Trust me. It's a big mistake. If you say something stupid, if he thinks you are an idiot, so what? He'll go find someone else, and someone who doesn't think you're stupid will be happy to spend time with you."

Sarah hung her head and resumed twirling the pink satin ribbon. Maddy sat her down on her bed. "Why did you decide to come to this school?"

Sarah gave her a funny look. "You don't remember?"

"Humor me."

"I wanted to get away from home...." Sarah began hesitantly.

"Because you hated your family?" Maddy asked, knowing the answer.

"No. Because I was born and raised in Antioch. I'd been to Seattle once before and loved it. I thought it would be a challenge to my faith to go to a secular school, and a personal challenge to be without my family."

"And you did it!" Maddy exclaimed.

Sarah smiled. "Yeah. I did."

"See, Sarah. You've got intelligence and strength. The only thing you lack is a sense of self-assurance with guys."

"And new people," Sarah added.

"You're getting better at that," Maddy encouraged.

Sarah's smile faded. "But what about guys? Am I ugly or something? Why hasn't a guy ever liked me?"

Maddy rolled her eyes and threw herself back on her bed. "Look at the facts. Number one—you're shy to begin with. Number two—you were very sheltered by your parents, *and* you went to a very small school. Number three—you probably haven't said more than ten words to any of the guys here. How can you expect one to like you if you never say a word?"

"Will you teach me, Maddy?"

"That will be my mission in life, Sarah," Maddy said in mock solemnity, her hand over her heart.

In a flash, Sarah found a pencil and heaved it at Maddy. "I'm not a charity case, okay?"

Maddy plopped on her own bed. "Okay."

Sarah left for the bathroom. Maddy took off her clothes and pulled on a baggy T-shirt and boxers. She climbed into bed with her Bible, hoping Sarah was talked out. The Bible still felt strange to her. The words didn't always make sense. Yet a hunger for God made her go back day after day. She had recently begun underlining all God's promises in green. That was helping her to understand at least a few words here and there.

She opened the Bible she'd bought with her own money. She always opened it the same way—as if it were fragile and might fall apart. She smoothed each page down until she came to a glossy page with gold scrolled letters. "This Bible Presented to:" In her best handwriting she had written her name. *Maddy Maria MacDonald*. "By:" Maddy had thought a long time about what to put here. She finally wrote, *Herself*. After thinking about it a little more, she had crossed out *Herself* and had written, *Her Father*.

Every time Maddy opened her Bible, she turned first to this page. She let her hand move down the glossy page, almost as if she could feel the letters she had written there. She had actually found God *and* admitted her sins, taking a long, deep bath in the blood of Jesus. She had committed her life to a new way of living more than a month earlier than the date inscribed in her Bible. It had taken her that long to earn the extra forty dollars she needed to buy it. But it was worth it. She never wanted to forget the commitment she made. Never wanted to forget the price someone paid for her to have a new life. God had gone to a lot of trouble to get this book to her. The least she could do was to read it and understand it the best she could.

Sarah returned quietly and climbed into her bed with a textbook. In no time, she had fallen asleep with her reading light on. Maddy had made it her bedtime ritual to slip Sarah's book out of her hands and onto the desk. She switched off the light as Sarah moaned and rolled over in her sleep.

Maddy crawled back into her own snug bed, trading her Bible for a library book. But before she opened it, she wanted to talk to God about Sarah, her family, and Jason. She didn't feel she knew a lot about prayer or being a Christian. But she did know this—she was already changing into a different person—more like a better version of herself than she really was.

60

Over the next week, Maddy settled into a routine. School in the morning and early afternoon. Library for four hours with Jason, her reluctant tutor. Study in the evenings.

"You have no social life," Sarah said Friday evening as she twirled in front of the mirror. "Do you think I ought to wear leggings more often?"

"I don't have time for a social life," Maddy replied, still looking at her English text. "And, yes. You look fabulous in leggings."

"Kick called again. He wants to know when you're going to get out and have some fun." Sarah opened her closet and stared into it.

"Tell him in about four years."

"Come on, Maddy. I think he likes you. If you don't pay attention to him, I might just have to steal him from you," Sarah teased.

Maddy leaned back in her chair, stretching her arms over her head. "I think he's great, too. But how in the world am I going to fit him into my schedule?"

"Maybe you'll have to make time." Sarah fingered a couple tops, obviously thinking hard about them.

"Okay," Maddy conceded. "Tell him to catch me at a meal. You know when I eat," Maddy said, picking up a 3 x 5 card to make another boring flash card. It seemed so juvenile, but it also seemed the only way she could learn some of this stuff.

"Well, too bad you aren't ready to party tonight." Sarah removed a pair of black slacks from the closet and held them up to her waist. She stuck her tongue out, then put them back in the closet.

Maddy looked up from the card, surprised. "You're going to a party alone?"

Sarah's face fell. "No. I meant too bad you aren't ready to party because I want you to go with me. I'm not ready to do this on my own."

"The Cup & Chaucer. Seven to midnight. That's my party."

"Can I come?"

After Sarah settled on jeans and a blouse with embroidery down the front, the two girls walked to the coffee house. Maddy wanted to ride her bike but Sarah had no wheels, so they walked.

Maddy got Sarah situated on a sofa where there was usually a lot of action. That way she would be forced to meet someone new. Then Maddy settled herself behind the bar to help Brad.

Throughout the evening, she looked at Sarah whenever she could. Each time the seats around Sarah were full, but Sarah was huddled into a corner of the sofa, her hand pressed to her mouth. Eventually, she disappeared, and Maddy forgot about her.

At closing, Maddy gathered up the garbage in a large plastic bag and took it out back. She opened the lid to the garbage pail, then paused. Someone was out there. She could feel their eyes, even though she couldn't see them. A prickly feeling crept up her spine. Slowly, she turned. Her hand tightened around the neck of the bag of garbage in case she needed a weapon. "Who's there?"

Silence answered her. She could still feel the eyes. "I know you're there." The damp alley smelled of ripe garbage, steamy coffee, and Chinese food from the restaurant at the end of the block.

A bent form in an old, ankle-length coat came out of the shadows of the alley. His hair and beard hadn't seen much care in at least a year. His face was darkened by dirt or sun, or both. Maddy figured that in Seattle, it had to be dirt. "Didn't mean to scare ya," the man said. His grin revealed missing teeth. What was left looked to be in dire need of dental care.

Maddy relaxed. "You waiting for this?" she asked, holding up the garbage bag.

"Anything good in it?" There was humbleness, yet strength in his voice.

"Maybe a few half-eaten brownies. Not much else." Maddy smiled. She wished she could give this man more.

He held out his hand. "Even one brownie would be good."

"You like coffee?" Maddy asked. The pungent smell of body odor and grime clung to the air. "We're closing. If I can get the rest before Brad dumps it...."

"Got more than one cup?" The man's thick eyebrows popped up, his brown eyes expectant.

Maddy looked around in the dark, but could only see dark building shapes. A few paths of light illuminated patches of darkness. "How many of you are there?"

"Three."

"Three cups of coffee it is." Maddy dashed inside.

"Brad. Don't empty the pots."

"Only one left," he said, gesturing toward the last pot of Franklin's French Roast.

"I'll take it."

Brad looked at her through narrowed eyes. "You've been out back?"

"It's okay." Maddy smiled hopefully, her eyes pleading.

"I don't want you to get hurt." Brad straightened his six-foot-four-inch frame, as if proving he'd be a bodyguard if necessary.

Maddy pushed her lips together. "Oh, quit it. Homeless people are mostly harmless—and hungry."

Brad pointed again to the large silver urn that had not been emptied. "Go on, take it. I want to get out of here." Maddy was able to coax two and a half cups out of it. "Next time I'm here, let me empty the urns," she suggested.

Brad shrugged his shoulders. "Makes no difference to me who empties them. Just so long as it gets done on time."

Maddy reached over and gave him a gentle punch on his arm. "Thanks."

She squashed the three Styrofoam cups together and took them out to the man outside. He and his two friends—one

64

female, one of uncertain gender—eagerly took the steaming cups from her. "Hope you don't get in trouble," the man said.

Maddy smiled. "It's worth the risk. I'm here weekends. Not always at closing. Do you hang out back here?"

"When it gets dark," the man said after gulping the hot coffee. Maddy wondered if he had any taste buds left.

"I'll try to bring you coffee when I can. No promises."

"Thanks."

"And I'll try to keep the leftover snacks separate," she added.

"You're an angel," the woman said, her voice cracking. She pulled her man-sized overcoat around several layers of dresses and sweaters. A pair of plaid polyester men's slacks poked out underneath.

Tell that to Jason, Maddy thought to herself. Out loud she said, "See you tomorrow."

As Maddy moved to walk out the front door, Brad stopped her. "Missing something?"

Maddy looked about herself. "I didn't bring my purse today. Thanks, anyway."

Brad smiled. "It's a little bigger than your purse."

Maddy felt confused. "I've got my cape. I don't wear gloves. What?"

Brad nodded with his head toward the back corner.

"I thought that light stayed on," Maddy said. "I'll turn it off if you want."

Brad pointed to a dark corner where Sarah had fallen asleep. "Your friend."

"Oops."

Maddy had thought she'd gone home, but she'd only moved. Gently, she shook Sarah. Although Sarah didn't seem to be fully awake, she responded to Maddy's urging.

As they walked back to campus, it surprised Maddy that the cops never stopped to see which one of them was drunk. Sleepy Sarah sure looked it, and Maddy didn't look much better, trying to hold her up. By the time they reached the dorms, Sarah had finally woken up enough to slog along by herself.

"You meet anyone special tonight?" Maddy asked her.

"I don't think so. Ask me tomorrow."

On Saturday morning, after her brief, weekly conversation with Gram, Maddy joined her roommate for breakfast at the cafeteria. "This time, watch where you're sitting," Maddy told Sarah as they took their loaded trays toward the dining room.

"Hey, babes, over here!" Both girls turned toward the voice.

Kick stood, waving his long two-tone blue felt cap over his head as if they couldn't see him.

"Saved a seat for you," he said as they drew near, smiling a huge grin at Maddy. "Been trying to find you all week."

"I'm always eating," Maddy said with a smile.

"Trying to become the fat lady at the circus?"

Something in Kick's tone made it sound like an attack. Maddy brushed the feeling off, figuring it was only his gruff way of trying to be funny. She pointed to his hat, which split into two triangles, its points dangling to his waist. "Are you trying out for the part of court jester?"

Kick flicked the ends. "I already won." He pointed at Maddy's plate. "That stuff is not healthy for you," he said. "I thought you were smarter than that."

"You're eating salad, too," Maddy protested.

"Ahh. But mine doesn't have fat calories soaking into every fiber." He leaned toward them and whispered, "My lettuce is naked. Yours is dressed. Remember, naked is always better."

Sarah blushed. Maddy raised her eyebrows. "That I won't forget."

"When you're done loading up on fat globules, want to go do something with me?" Kick grinned widely, his brown eyes eager.

Maddy tilted her head and looked at Kick through slitted eyes. She ignored Sarah's under-the-table jabs.

"Actually, I have to study then go to work."

"At?"

"The Cup & Chaucer."

Kick nodded. "Cool place. Skip the studies for one day."

Maddy flashed through all the things she needed to do in her head. Then there was Gram's voice loud and clear. "Not today."

"When?"

"If we plan it right, I could go next Saturday between lunch and work."

"Then plan it right. In the meantime, I shall wish to see thy lovely face at each meal." He looked at her with such anticipation, that in spite of some misgivings, Maddy was charmed.

Maddy found her work to be easy. The ebb and flow of customers didn't faze her. When it was slow, she cleaned Joe

Plimco's books. When it was busy, she was behind the bar, or cleaning off tables, or chatting with the people who sat alone.

"We need more snacks to offer people," she said out of the blue one day to Brad.

"Where'd that come from?" Brad planted his large hands on the bar.

Maddy shrugged. "I look at these people and think they'd drink more coffee if they had stuff to snack on. Snacks make you thirsty. Thirst means more coffee sales."

"What kind of snacks? Desserts? We already have some stuff."

"Maybe one or two more choices. But more healthy stuff. Bran muffins. Health cookies."

Brad thumped one hand on the counter. "You mean food that will be more healthy for your homeless friends." He smiled.

Maddy smiled back. "If they benefit, that's great."

"Health food has no preservatives, Maddy," he stated, knowing full well she already knew this. "That means we have to get rid of them quicker if they aren't eaten."

Maddy smiled and took a wet rag to clean coffee spills. "Oh, really?" she said after a moment.

Brad threw another damp rag and hit her in the back of the head.

A burst of customers distracted them, the first in a steady stream that kept them going for a long time.

"Maddy," Brad said, as he wiped the counter during their first breather. "Check this guy out." He jerked his head toward a table in the corner. "He comes in and sits alone a lot."

Maddy leaned on the counter to get a better look. A clean-cut country boy observed the room around him. "He doesn't look sad and lonely. It looks like he *wants* to be alone."

"Why?" Brad asked. He looked at her as though he knew the answer, but wanted to know what she thought.

"He's checking everybody out. Like he's interested. He's an observer." Maddy said.

"You should go talk to him."

"Okay," Maddy chirped. She knew Brad didn't really mean it. That's why she went.

"Hi," Maddy said, sitting in a chair opposite the newcomer. His brown eyes were framed with round, wire-rimmed glasses, and his blond hair was shorter than that of most of the guys she knew. "I hope I'm not intruding or anything."

The guy shook his head, not really looking at her, but not looking away, either. He seemed like a little kid who had gotten caught eavesdropping.

"My name's Maddy," she said, sticking out her hand.

"Ethan," he said in a soft voice.

"You go to the U?"

Ethan nodded.

Maddy paused a moment, thoroughly checking him out. "Me, too. You're not from around here, are you?"

Ethan shook his head.

"Me, either, really." They both sat, silent. Maddy wasn't sure what to say to Ethan. She figured he was too shy to speak to her. She took a breath and tried a dumb question. "Where are you from?"

"Grew up in the Smokies."

"The Smokies," Maddy said thoughtfully. "We drove through them. Quiet. Peaceful. Hardly anyone around."

Ethan nodded again. He waved his hand toward the crowded coffee house. "We didn't have this many people in church on Sunday. And everyone came."

Now it was Maddy's turn to nod. "That's why you're sitting in the corner, watching everyone like a hawk."

A small, sincere smile crept over Ethan's calm face. He nodded. "Hawks observe from a distance for good reason."

"To better stake out their prey."

Ethan's grin grew. "Just to make sure they know what dangers and opportunities are out there."

The front door gave an angry jingle. A booming voice crossed the tavern. "Maddy! You two-timing me already?" Maddy turned to see Kick gobbling up the space between them with long strides. "And he's a geek!"

Maddy shrunk inside herself, horrified that Kick would verbally trounce this poor, shy guy.

"Hey, Maddy. I thought you had better taste than that," he continued.

Ethan looked startled at first. Then he shook his head and looked away, ignoring Kick.

Maddy touched Ethan's arm. "He thinks he's funny. I'm sorry." She stood to meet Kick face to face, glaring at him. "What can I get you?"

Kick dropped to his knees. "Come with me, baby. Come to the party of the century, and we will laugh and dance the night away."

Glancing around the coffee house, Maddy saw and felt the glares of the other customers. "Shush."

"I shan't stand until you answer yes." He flung his arms out to add to the dramatic effect.

"Yes—*after* I'm off work."

"Okay," Kick said in a normal voice. He stood up and winked at Ethan. Then he strode back across the tavern to the table most people didn't like. It was too close to the door, too close to the coffee bar, and too close to the cash register.

For the next couple hours, Kick sat there, making comments to people and about people. Brad became strangely silent. Gradually, Maddy loosened up and laughed at much that Kick said. She threw quips back at him when she could. Kick almost always laughed. When he didn't, he'd tug on his goatee and give her a funny look.

Maddy insisted on cleaning up after everyone. That way she could save all the half-eaten food for her friends out back. When it was closing time, she disappeared out the back with her three cups of coffee.

"Thanks, ma'am," the bushy man said to her. "My name's Duckworth. It would be a pleasure to know yours."

"Maddy MacDonald."

"Gina," said the woman.

"Terry," said the third, still not giving a clue to its gender.

"Oh, I almost forgot," Maddy said, fishing in her apron pocket. "Here." She held out a napkin with several pieces of brownie and cake in it.

"Have you gotten yourself kidnapped?" came a booming voice behind her. Maddy didn't have to look this time. She knew it was Kick. Those in front of her scattered into the shadows. "Brad told me to leave you alone. I told him to bite it. What are you doing out here?"

"Just taking care of closing business."

"Who were those awful-looking people?"

Maddy laughed. "You look quite a bit like they do."

"No way." Kick made a face.

Maddy walked around Kick and went back inside. He followed, talking almost in her ear as she went. "I hope you aren't feeding bums or anything, Maddy. They need to learn to take care of themselves. There really is no such thing as a homeless person. If they don't want to live like the rest of us, that's too bad."

"Kick. If you don't stop, I'm not going to the party with you tonight."

Kick put his hands up as if to protect himself. "Okay, okay. But don't say I didn't warn you."

Maddy bit the inside of her cheek, wondering if she *should* go to the party. She let her thoughts zip through all she knew of Kick—which wasn't a whole lot yet. He was truly funny most of the time. But sometimes his humor crossed her boundaries of what was okay. She was certain he didn't mean to be cruel. He just didn't know when to stop.

Maddy glanced at him while she cleaned up. She sighed. *I guess he really just needs a few lessons in social graces.*

7

Maddy could hear the music before she could see the large, old house it came from. She had left her bike at The Cup & Chaucer, or "The Cup" as she had learned regulars called it, so she could walk with Kick. Holding his hand, she started to move with the music.

Kick grinned. "Oooh, baby, move those hips."

Maddy looked up at Kick's brown eyes, ignoring his suggestive comment. "You sure it's okay for us to go to this party?"

"I'm invited, so you're invited."

Familiar feelings began to descend upon Maddy. The trickle of excitement crawled up her spine. The energizing impulses raced to her limbs. The exhilaration stimulated her brain. By the time the door opened, spilling light across the wooden front porch and weed-choked front lawn, Maddy was ready to party.

Recognizing no one, she eagerly smiled and said hello to everyone. Kick introduced her to a few people here and there. Most of the kids looked like Kick—long-haired guys with patched jeans, some with sport caps on backwards. Many had pierced ears. Still, some of the kids looked like direct PCU descendants in casual, normal stuff—clean jeans, middle-of-the-road hair—not preppie short, or hippie long. Long enough to be loose, short enough to hang somewhere around the ear-lobe. Some of the girls seemed out of place. Sarah types. Very clean, very innocent. Maddy had missed the part of the evening where they were all wide-eyed and nervous. Now they carried their beer, or Coke and vodka, or wine without hesitation.

"Come on, Kick, let's dance."

"I want a beer first."

"Dance first, beer later." Maddy hoped she could distract him from the alcohol as long as possible. She took him by the hand and dragged him to the center of the living room where many other bodies were also moving to the vibrating music. Kick drew her close. The warmth and strength of his chest brought a smile to her face. Out of the blue, she thought about Jesus and what he would think about her being there, then quickly shoved the thought away.

She snuggled against Kick, remembering so many others in the past. The comfort they brought. The warmth. Without a doubt, Maddy knew that she wanted a man in her life. Someone to hold her. Comfort her. Be strong for her. She melted into Kick, letting every stress flow out of her. Gone were Jason and his unrealistic expectations. Gone was the strain of trying to understand Biology. Gone was any need to study, or even pass. And here was a man to hold her.

"Song's over. Time for my beer," Kick announced. He turned so abruptly, Maddy lost her balance.

"Shame you can't hold your alcohol better," someone said to her disdainfully.

74

Maddy followed Kick into the kitchen where the drinks littered the counter, stuck out of ice-filled, tin wash basins on the floor, and lined the four refrigerators. "Beer?" Kick asked over his shoulder.

Maddy shook her head. She stared at the vodka, longing for just one short trip into the past. She spun on her heels and went back to the smoke-filled living room. She shook the desire from inside her and started swaying to the music.

How can this be bad? She wondered. *It's fun. It makes me feel so incredibly wonderful. Nothing bad ever happened at parties before. Did it?*

Maddy felt a hand slide around the front of her waist. "Dance some more?"

She nodded and turned, finding that place of peace again as she nestled against Kick's chest. Sometimes he dropped his chin on top of her head. Maddy didn't think beyond the moment, which she felt would never end.

After Kick downed three beers, he'd also had enough of dancing. They found a sofa, making a spot wide enough for one into a cozy spot for two. Maddy snuggled down on Kick's lap and into his shoulder.

"I could party every night," Kick said. "There's so much life here." He held his beer aloft in salute to his friends who passed.

"Ummm. Me too," Maddy said dreamily. Inside, she knew she should leave. *This is part of my past,* she reminded herself.

Just once, Maddy protested silently. *Just once won't hurt. I won't do it all. Just this much.*

"Leave," something inside her urged. "Leave now."

Maddy snuggled even deeper into Kick, hoping that would

make her thoughts go away.

"Kick," she asked, pointing her mouth to his ear so she wouldn't have to shout over the music. "Do you think God cares whether or not we're at a party?"

Kick made a face. He put his mouth to her ear. "Why should I care what God thinks?"

Maddy felt confused. "But you were at the church rally last week."

Kick shrugged. "So? So were a lot of other people here."

Maddy had to agree. "Don't you believe in God?"

"Sorta. I guess there's a God. But I don't think about him much."

Maddy put her arm around Kick's neck to make it easier to talk. She fought off feelings of disappointment. "Why did you go to the church?" she asked carefully.

"To meet people. Isn't that what the invitation said? Come meet people from school? So I did. And boy did I walk off with first prize." Kick kissed her cheek and turned his attention to the dance floor.

"Would you go back?"

"Only if they had another cool party. To church, though? No." He paused a moment, then turned to her again. "I love meeting people. I love having a good time. Whatever's going on that will open those doors—I'm there!"

Maddy nodded. She understood that. Her thoughts drifted to past parties. To her former way of life. In all the high schools she went to, there was the easy way to make friends, and there was the hard way. The hard way was to try to break into cliques that only wanted people that looked or talked like them. The easy way to make friends was to go to a party.

Maddy looked around the room, remembering all that had ended when she became a Christian. As a new believer, she learned quickly that her old life had to go. And in the joy of knowing Christ, she had eagerly said good-bye.

Now her eagerness was fading. She'd forgotten how comforting a cloud of cigarette smoke could be. The smell of alcohol on every breath. The slow loosening of the boundaries people tightly cloaked themselves with as talk began to flow.

"Can we dance some more?" she begged Kick.

He nodded. She slid off his lap and held out her hand to help him stand. Then, as she danced, other old feelings began to wake up. She wanted to be closer to Kick. Very close.

She looked up at him. He chatted nonstop about this person and that person. "Be quiet," she said lowly.

He looked at her, confused. He was quiet for a split second, then started his monologue again.

"Enough." She gazed up at him intently. And he complied with a long kiss. She didn't stop him, fully enjoying the kiss.

"Come here," he said in a husky voice, and led her from the dance floor. He moved down the hallway to a back room. Someone opened the door and slid through it.

Maddy felt struck with something powerful. "Incredible," she said, inhaling deeply. "That is the most wonderful fragrance ever discovered by man."

"It's pot," Kick said, looking hesitant.

Maddy gave him a full smile. "I know. Isn't it wonderful?" She knew her eyes sparkled. She could feel that complete joy from the past.

A surprised smile took over Kick's face. "Go in?"

Maddy nodded. People scooted to widen the circle. She placed herself next to Kick, cross-legged on the floor. She watched the joint being passed toward them, anticipating the warm and wonderful feelings she would soon experience. Kick inhaled deeply, held his breath until he could hold it no longer, then exhaled. He passed the joint to Maddy.

Maddy held it, caught up by the experiential knowledge of what would happen next. The peace. The new joy of eating. Physical pleasures.

"NO!" The thought exploded in her head.

Quickly, Maddy passed the joint on, feeling suddenly afraid of it, as if it were a lion that would pounce on her and kill her.

She stood, suddenly trembling. "I'm sorry. I forgot. I can't."

Kick reached up and touched her arm.

"I want to, I really do. But I *can't*." Maddy said to him. "I'll get kicked out of school. I have to leave. Now."

"Who's gonna know?" someone in the circle asked. "Those neurotics try to run our lives as it is. Since when did someone get kicked out for smoking a little pot?"

Tears threatened to ruin what little composure she had left. "I'm here special. I can't do drugs at all." Her breathing came more rapidly.

"Come on, Maddy. Stay for me. Just keep me company," Kick pleaded.

Maddy turned and fled the room. Her heart beat wildly. How could she want something so wrong? What if Admin even found out she'd been at the party? Would she be kicked out then?

She made her way to the kitchen, where she found a carton of orange juice and several bottles of vodka on the counter. For a moment, Maddy thought about pouring herself a screwdriver. But the same instincts that kept her from taking the joint caused her to refrain. A moment later, Kick appeared from nowhere. "Come back, Maddy. I don't want people to think I've got a straight girlfriend."

The noise and smells began to get to Maddy. Her brain felt fuzzy. "I can't, Kick. I can't."

"You're not so into this God thing that you can't have fun, are you?"

Maddy shook her head and stared at the bottle of vodka again.

In a moment, too much became too confusing. She took Kick by the hand and led him outside the back door. The fall night, crisp and cold, hid stars behind a cloak of clouds. "If I screw up," she told him, "God will forgive me. But the Admin won't." Inside she felt sick, like she'd just deeply hurt her best friend. The feeling confused her even more.

Kick nodded. "Cool. Just so long as I understand."

But he didn't. Maddy knew he didn't and never tried to correct him.

"I'm going home," she said.

"It's only two. We've got hours before daylight."

"I'm going home." Maddy turned and went inside. It took her another fifteen minutes to find her cape. She put it on and fled down the front stairs, feeling like an unhappy Cinderella.

The music followed her into the night.

She wished she could cry. She wished she knew why she

wanted to cry. The emptiness of the party consumed her. Images flashed repeatedly across the inside of her mind. When the lights came on and the party was over, what would be left? A lot of headaches, stomachaches, and regrets. Lots of those kids back there would weather the aftermath just fine. Others would find heartaches to match the groaning protests of the rest of their bodies.

"But it *is* fun," she told herself. "I had a ball until God butted in." She wanted to ignore the Cosmic Killjoy. But she couldn't. Something in her *had* changed when she told Christ she'd live a new way. She couldn't call God a Cosmic Killjoy, because she knew he only wanted what was best for her. And for some reason, that scene back there was not best.

She stuck her tongue out at God.

Once in her room, she could smell all the sordid odors that clung to her. Cigarette smoke. Pot. Alcohol. Other stuff she couldn't place. Instead of falling exhausted into bed like she wanted to, she trudged to the shower and scrubbed herself clean from her head to her toes.

Y ou going to church, Maddy?" Sarah stuck her face close to
Maddy's. She smelled of soap and Obsession.

"Not with you," Maddy grumped.

Sarah stood, putting her hands on her hips. "Well, thanks a
lot."

Maddy rolled over on her back, squinting against the sun-
light. "I meant I'm not going to that church any more. I'm going
to the one we went to for the party last week."

Sarah relaxed. "Well, okay. Can I go with you sometime?"

"Yeah." Maddy pushed herself into a half-sitting position.
"See you later, huh?"

Maddy showered again before going to church. Then she
looked all through her closet for something appropriate to
wear, but could find nothing where the top half met the bottom
half. In the end, Maddy put on a long, flowered print skirt and
a plain, cropped sweater. She left her belly chain on the desk.
She tucked her feet into flats and her wrists into her bracelets.
Without using a brush to smooth her hair, she pulled the front
pieces back into an alligator clip.

She had originally planned to attend the college department
class, but now she knew she couldn't face anyone. What if they

had gone to the party? What if someone had told them that Maddy had gone to the party? She preferred the anonymity of the worship service. Besides, she felt she needed time to face God alone.

The usher, Bill Wilson, smiled at her and pointed out where his wife was sitting so Maddy could join them again.

Maddy shook her head, giving him only the hint of a smile. "I need to be where I can worship alone," she told him.

He nodded, understanding. "In that case, you'll want to sit right down there." He pointed to a section off to one side. "Most people avoid that spot, 'cause you can't see the preacher real well."

"Thanks."

Maddy sat in a pew, tucking her feet underneath her. Would Bill be nice to her if he knew? She looked around the church. People of all sorts walked in, found a seat, and sat down. Only a small handful seemed like they were capable of doing anything wrong. Or anything unusual.

Maddy bowed her head to block out the view of all the people. She needed to sort through her thoughts without distraction. She wished she had brought her Bible, remembering suddenly that she hadn't read it in several days.

Mentally, she retraced the events of the night before, wondering what made her so confused. What upset her so much.

In her mind, she danced again with Kick. It had felt so peaceful to be in a man's arms. *It didn't matter who. It mattered only that he was male.*

No, she argued with herself. *I like Kick. He's cool. He lets me be myself.*

She pushed those thoughts away and found herself in the room where everyone was getting high. In that room, she hadn't minded if God was upset. She hadn't minded if she hurt God. She only minded that she might get caught and be thrown out of school.

Finally, the tears started to come. Just little, slow-paced ones. One rolled down her cheek before another escaped her eye.

How can you claim to love someone so much, yet not care if you hurt him or not?

Did Maddy really love God? Did it really hurt God if she went to parties? She tried to picture Jesus there. That part seemed okay. He loved everyone. What didn't fit were the images of Jesus dancing slowly, seductively, with someone. Or Jesus toking on a joint. Or Jesus guzzling beer and being silly. If he was her role model, then the party couldn't be right.

The worship began. Maddy couldn't sing or pray. If there had been a way for her to make an easy escape, she would have. As soon as the closing song began, Maddy bolted. She skipped lunch, going straight to bed. When she woke, there were five pink phone messages posted on the corkboard wall by the front door. All from Kick. She tossed them in the trash on her way out the door to work.

Maddy poured herself into her tasks at The Cup. Brad tried to stir her up, tease her, get her talking. She forced superficial smiles once an hour just to keep Brad thinking it was PMS that flung her into a bad mood overnight.

"Hey! My little Zulicka! My belly dancer!" a voice said behind her hours later. "Are you ready to party tonight?" Maddy didn't turn around. She continued wiping up coffee rings from the table in front of her.

A moment later, a strong arm looped around her waist and spun her around. Kick moved seductively side to side mimicking their slow dance of the night before. "Come on, Maddy. Whaddya say?"

"Kick!" Maddy said, saying his name in tones that ran up and down the scale. She pushed him away. "Not here. I'm working." He disgusted her. He reminded her how disgusted she was with herself.

"Not forever." His arm came out like a hook, ready to catch her again. Maddy dodged it, heading toward the bar. Kick followed her, throwing the upper half of his body over the bar. His face peered over the other side. "Say yes, Madds. Say you'll go."

His goofy face and pleading caught Maddy off-guard. Maybe she was being too hard on him. His behavior the night before was no different than hers had been at countless high school parties. She started to smile for real. "No, you idiot. I have school tomorrow. And so do you."

"And this will put me in the perfect mood for facing up to old Mrs. Sickeningberger."

"Her name is Hickenberger." Maddy wiped coffee spots off Brad's prized copper espresso machine with a clean, dry cloth.

"Whatever. You have to come. We'll have fun again."

Brad came up and crouched between them. "Just say no, Maddy."

"I didn't know your dad was right here in Seattle, Madds." Kick glared at Brad.

"He's not." Maddy put her hand in Brad's face and gently pushed on it. "Butt out, Brad." He stood, shrugging his shoulders.

Maddy then turned to Kick. "No," she said softly.

"No? You can't say no," Kick told her.

Maddy stuck her face close to his feeling stronger by the minute. "I just did. No, no, no, no."

Kick slid off the bar and put his hands up to his ears. "AAAAAggghhh. I can't hear this." Maddy had to duck her head to hide her smile. In spite of her concerns about Kick, she was charmed.

Brad rolled his eyes. "Maddy. Can you do something about him? He's scaring the customers."

Maddy stepped around the bar and opened the front door. "Bye, Kick."

He heaved a big sigh. "You won't reconsider?" He batted big puppy dog eyes at her.

"Bye, Kick." Maddy tried to play her part well, forcing her smile to remain hidden.

"Lunch tomorrow?" Kick asked in a little boy voice.

Maddy nodded, still holding back her smile.

Kick stood tall. "She said yes. I got her to say yes." And he walked out as a dignified man.

"He's nuts," Brad said, watching Kick move past the windows.

"Yeah," Maddy said, half-smiling.

"Hey, is that a real smile?"

"Real, baby. Real." Maddy let go and flashed him a huge grin.

That night as she got ready for bed, Maddy's heart didn't feel so heavy. Kick's bizarre attitude and appearance at The Cup & Chaucer smothered the horrible feelings she had about herself and her recent decisions. She buzzed about the room, gathering her work for the next day. Sarah bumped through the door carrying a basket full of clean laundry, which she dumped on the bed in a heap.

"Good party Saturday night?" Sarah asked.

Conflicting feelings raced through Maddy. Hot and cold. Good and bad. Enjoyment and guilt. "It was a party," she replied, shrugging her shoulders.

"I'd like to go with you sometime." Sarah scooped up all her socks and underwear and threw them into one drawer. "All the parties I've ever been to were so predictable. There's some stupid ice-breaker, even though we all know each other. There's a couple dumb games, then everyone eats and talks. Wowie zowie. Cool and groovy. Swell. I'm thrilled." She sat on her bed in the middle of the warm laundry. "I know meeting people is not what I do best. But I'd still like to experience a little of life."

Maddy pretended to be digging through her closet for something, although she was actually trying to cope with the flashing images in her brain. Putting sweet Sarah at the party. Trying to place her somewhere where she fit. "That kind of party doesn't sound so bad," Maddy said, her voice muffled by the clothes.

Sarah tried to explain. "I want to grow up. I want to be

myself. I don't want to be a clone of my family and classmates. I don't know how to figure all this out."

Maddy backed out of the closet and sat on a pile of shoes lined up outside. "You're saying you want me to help you find yourself?"

"Yeah!"

Maddy shook her head. "No one can do that for you."

Sarah sighed and grabbed a red sweatshirt to fold. She gave it a quick snap. "I know. But I'd rather have a guided tour of this new world than blunder in all by myself. I figure I'll make fewer mistakes that way."

Maddy picked lint off her leggings. "I guess that makes sense." She still hoped she could get Sarah to have her "world tour" without parties.

"My first goal is to do something about my clothes. I had to wear uniforms all my school days. My mom picked out and bought most of my weekend clothes from Mervyn's clearance sales. I don't even know what I like to wear."

Maddy picked up one of her flats and scraped mud off the side of it with her thumbnail. "Okay. Tuesday, let's go shopping. I'll take you to my favorite rag shop. You can shop 'til you drop and still not pay that much money. I'm warning you though, most of these clothes are not very traditional."

"I'm tired of traditional," Sarah said brightly. "That's what I've been trying to tell you."

"That is incredibly disgusting," Sarah said.

Maddy turned the tiger-print leggings around. "I don't know

about that, Sarah. You have to learn to be daring. Learn to be you."

Sarah shook her head. "I'm not so sure that's me."

"Rowwww," Kick purred in her ear. "One sexy little kitten is going to slip into those things."

Sarah dropped her chin and looked at him. "I don't think so. At least it won't be me."

"This," Maddy teased while holding up a silver studded bustier, "will make every man turn his head."

Sarah nodded slowly as if she was not quite sure whether Maddy was joking, but was certainly sure that she didn't want every man to turn his head.

"I like this," she finally said, holding up a flowered blouse.

"Excuse me?" Kick put his hand up as if shading his eyes. He scanned the whole store. "Is this the K-Mart blue light special? Is my grandmother here in disguise?" He slapped his hands to his cheeks, his mouth making a surprised O. He stared at Sarah, then threw his arms into the air. He hugged her and started jumping up and down. "Grandma, oh, Grandma! I'm so happy I got to see you. I've missed you so much. Tell me this one thing." He held Sarah at arm's length. "Is it real hot there? Or did you get to go to the nice place with pearls on the gates?"

Sarah whacked him. "Okay, okay. I get the hint. I'll keep looking."

Maddy put on one of her pretend smiles. "How's this?"

Sarah looked at the tailored black skirt. "Now, that's not bad."

"Ah-hah!" Maddy said. "I caught you. Don't tell me you want different. This is as straight as they come."

Sarah snatched it from Maddy before she had a chance to place it back on the rack. "You told me I would find only good stuff here."

"Okay. So I lied. They don't only have good stuff. They have some gruesome stuff, too."

"Oh, ladies! Over here!" Kick sang in a high little voice. Over his clothes, he modeled a tiny piece of lingerie.

"K-i-c-k," Sarah said, blushing.

"Oh, well." He whipped it off and went on looking.

"We are getting nowhere," Maddy announced. They close in one hour, and I have to work on my biology report tonight."

"It's time for serious business." Kick turned his attention to the racks, flying through the clothes so quickly, there was no way he could see what passed by. "Very serious business."

"Stop it!" shrieked Maddy. "You're making my sides hurt."

Just then, she heard a familiar voice at the front of the store. "Do you have any jeans that aren't too worn? Or flannel shirts?"

Maddy turned toward the sound. Her laughter died the moment her brain made the connection. The shop girl was directing Jason to the spot where Maddy stood. Maddy looked down and saw she had the sleeve of a flannel shirt between her fingers. A burning coal would have lasted longer between her fingers than that sleeve.

"Buying more of your tawdry clothes?" Jason asked, as he approached her.

"No," Maddy said, her voice stumbling. "We're here for my roommate," she added without thinking.

Jason shook his head sadly, as if to say: "One sinner leads the other to fall."

"So why are you here?" Kick asked. "If this is the tawdry shop, then perhaps we could classify you in the tawdry way, too?"

Jason's face lost his color. He marched back to the shop girl. "I'll come back later when the store isn't so crowded."

Maddy felt weak.

"Jerk." Kick said.

Sarah gasped. "He really doesn't like you, does he?"

Maddy shook her head. "He's right."

"What'd you say?" Sarah asked.

Kick put his arm around her and hustled her toward the door. "Out of the way, everyone," he said to the clothes. "Out of the way. This young lady needs a bit of fresh air. She's suffocating in lies!"

Once outside, Kick started to fan her as if she were a fragile lady about ready to faint. Maddy smiled and started to laugh. "You are such a goon."

He bowed deeply. "At your service." He then stood, his hands on his hips, looking fiercely in all directions. "Where is that cad? I shall have his head on a platter for you."

"It's okay," Maddy said, putting her hand on Kick's arm. "Let's just forget it."

Kick shook his head in disgust. "Where do you pick up these toads, Maddy? Don't you have any taste at all? You're too nice to people and look what that gets you. Walked on."

Maddy felt her head spin. Kick's words bit into her as much as Jason's had. "Sarah is lost in the clothing wilderness," Maddy said, trying to change the subject. "We'd better go on a…on a…."

"It's called a 'rescue mission,' Maddy. Sheesh. Sometimes I wonder how you got into this university."

Maddy looked up to see Jason standing outside the yogurt store five feet away. He looked startled, his gaze focused on the back of Kick's head this time, rather than on Maddy. Maddy opened the door to the clothing shop and ducked in, Kick following close behind.

9

It was over a week before the three of them ran into Jason again. At lunch, Kick looked at Maddy, then across the room, then at Maddy once more. "Why does that guy keep staring at you? What's his problem?"

Maddy shrugged.

Sarah swallowed her pasta. "Maddy works with him. He hates her."

Kick looked from one to the other again. "That guy from the store? Is that so? You want me to fix him, Maddy?"

Maddy rolled her eyes and shook her head. "Yeah, let's give him another reason to hate me."

"I'll go talk to him. I promise not to punch him out," Kick offered, rubbing his fists one at a time.

"You can't fix it," Maddy said. "Don't try." She continued to eat her dry salad, hating every boring bite.

"You can't just let this go, Madds. Something has to be done," Kick pleaded.

"Kick. I've tried."

"You didn't have me before." Kick stared at Jason.

Maddy threw Sarah an "oh, brother" look. Then she looked directly at Kick. "I know you're trying to be nice. I know you are quite capable. But this is my problem, and I can handle it."

"Why does he hate you, anyway?" Kick asked, keeping his eyes on Jason.

Jason lifted his tray and started to walk toward them. Maddy figured he had to notice Kick looking at him. But if he did, he sure didn't show it.

"He hates the way I dress," Maddy told him. Voicing it sounded ridiculous.

"Well, I think some of what you put together is pretty stupid, too, but I don't hate you for it."

Jason walked by at that moment on his way to bus his tray. His eyes narrowed as he looked at Kick. Without a word, he walked on by.

The Wednesday before Thanksgiving, Kick left right after his last class, hopping a bus to Issaquah where his family lived. Sarah caught a ride to the airport and flew to Oakland, California, where her family would pick her up and drive her home to Antioch.

After they had gone, the campus lost much of its warmth, life, and flavor for Maddy. The very buildings looked sad and forlorn.

Despite her misgivings, by the next morning, Maddy was ready to tackle her weekend at Gram's. She set off on her bike beneath an inconsistent cloud cover, feeling inconsistent emotions about the long days ahead. Puget Sound glimmered whenever the clouds parted to reveal the sun and a brilliant blue sky.

Maddy had stuffed her bike's large, front flat basket with two small canvas bags that held her toiletries. She'd safety-pinned a map of Seattle to the top of one bag, then balanced the rear saddle baskets with books and clothes. Maddy loved the spectacle she made on the rattletrap old bike with her black cape flying behind her, her red hair a striking contrast as it flipped up in the wind. The bike clanked with every revolution of the pedals, sounding as if it might fall apart at any moment.

Storefronts and churches made way for houses, then office buildings. The old mixed with the modern, all of it a new world to Maddy. She got so caught up in the sights, there was no room to be nervous.

Then the fear hit her, all at once, as she rode up the drive to her grandmother's stately brick home at the top of First Hill. Maddy coasted to the front door and lowered her kickstand. Her heart beat in funny, rapid beats that almost seemed to twitter up near her throat. Her breathing came rapid and shallow. Maddy pulled the cape around the front of her. She smoothed her hair, then with a better thought, opened a canvas bag and made good use of the brush she dug out of the jumble.

Standing at the front door, she tried to decide whether she should ring the doorbell or just walk in. Deciding that knocking would be the perfect announcement, she grasped the brass lion's head and brought it down soundly on the knocker plate. She heard her Gram call to someone inside, but couldn't make out the words. The heavy door opened without a sound.

And there stood Jason.

Maddy swallowed and put on a smile. She took a step toward him. "Well, hello! Fancy meeting you here!" She put out her hand to shake his.

"This isn't funny," Jason said, closing the door partially.

"Hey. I didn't plan this."

Jason looked at her through narrowed eyes.

Maddy cocked her head. "I'm not stupid. I was looking forward to a weekend without you."

"You still could. You could turn around and leave right now. I'll tell Mrs. MacDonald it was just someone who got lost."

"That wouldn't work— "

"You just don't want it to work. Mrs. MacDonald is a kind, sweet woman. I don't think she'd really want to have a person like you here."

A true smile replaced the fake one. Maddy understood. Jason thought she was a guest! Well…she'd just let the truth remain unspoken until Jason figured it out for himself!

At that moment, Gram's face came into view, "Let her in, Jason!" Gram drew Maddy into her arms, then pushed her away to look at her. "I'm so glad you're here."

She wanted to say she was glad to be there, too. Considering the circumstances, Maddy wished she were anywhere else, so her only honest answer could be, "Thank you."

Gram took another look at her. "Didn't you bring your stuff to spend the weekend?"

Maddy ignored the hard look Jason gave her. "I left it on my bike."

"Well go get it before it gets rained on! And park your bike in the back. No sense in leaving it out front where someone might steal it."

"Not that anyone would want to," Maddy said with a chuckle triggered partially by the ludicrous image of someone stealing her old bike, partially by the wonderful thought that Jason had no clue this was her grandmother.

Maddy rolled her bike around to the rear, where she saw Jason's motorcycle. She parked her own bike underneath the canopy cover near the back door, then went to check out the damage on Jason's motorcycle. One side stood pristine and classy. She edged around the other side. There, she saw a dented, scraped mess.

"I had the handle and kickstand replaced," Jason said, standing on the rear porch. "I couldn't drive it without fixing those."

"I'm really sorry it happened," Maddy said. She looked up at him. "In more ways than one."

"I've wanted you to apologize," Jason said after a moment of silence.

Maddy sighed. "I have. I did. That day and since."

"You always end your apologies with, 'It was an *accident*.'"

Maddy danced her fingers lightly over the damaged gas tank. "It *was* an accident. I never meant to hurt you, or anyone else. I was enjoying the wind in my hair, the beautiful day...." She looked into his eyes. "I am truly sorry. If I could fix your bike, I would."

Jason leaned on the porch railing and looked over the top of her head to the manicured gardens. His eyes glazed over, darting back and forth. Maddy supposed he was reviewing that day in his head. She honored his silence and waited until he was ready to speak.

His words came out soft and gentle, like Maddy supposed the rest of him to be when he wasn't around her. "I accept your apology. It's difficult for me to say that, because I still have this picture of a wild woman coming toward me, dressed like the ultimate heathen, claiming to be a Christian. And to top it all off, you caused me to damage the one thing in life I have to be proud of."

Maddy nodded.

"I still don't approve of you," Jason added. "I don't think you realize how you are hurting the truth of the message we are supposed to bring to the lost."

"And I think that my looks have nothing to do with it. Maybe people who wouldn't listen to you, would listen to me."

"Females, maybe. But males would have other things on their mind."

A burst of laughter caught Maddy by surprise. "Oh, come on. That's a joke."

Jason blushed. "I'm not kidding. I just think you're giving the wrong impression."

Maddy shook her head. She grabbed her things and pushed past him into the house. "I'm not into impressions. I'm into life."

She marched through the screened porch and into the warm kitchen. "It smells wonderful. After I put my stuff away, I'm going to help you."

Gram kissed her on the cheek. "That will be wonderful, dear." She went back to pinching pie crust into a fluted edge.

Maddy shifted her load of stuff so she wouldn't drop any of it. "Same room?" she asked, wanting to get settled.

"You remember which one it is?"

"The prettiest one in the house."

Maddy loved Gram's house. Everything about it stirred longings within her. Deep stirrings of something lost, something needed. She moved slowly through the back hallway, her steps muffled by the deep wool floor covering. She loved the stairway best, with its crimson carpet, laid upon wooden stairs and held in place by brass rods. The mahogany banister curved upward, supported by turned posts.

Maddy tried to imagine her father running up and down these steps. Sliding down the banister. Pounding through the house with his friends following him. The images never formed completely. She could only picture him hiding under the stairs, trying to draw and draw and draw—obsessively drawing, but not knowing what. A restless drawing—almost frantic. That's the only father she could imagine. It's the only father she knew.

Upstairs, at the third room on the right, Maddy put her stuff down and opened the door. Every time she went into this room, she smiled. A real canopy bed—not one of the tacky ones made in the sixties—dominated the room. The mattress sat so high, Maddy always felt like a little girl when she climbed up on it. A down comforter underneath the bedspread gave the bed a lumpy, inviting look. A priscilla-curtained window looked out over the gardens in the back. A window seat stretched beneath it. She loved the cushion, pillows, and teddy bears Gram placed there.

Maddy opened the closet by its crystal knob and dumped

her stuff on the floor. She wanted to unpack and put her things on the antique wash stand. But the smells from the kitchen wafted into her room and reminded her she had priorities.

Gram had put Jason to work peeling potatoes.

"We're having a discussion, Maddy. Mashed potatoes or scalloped?"

"What does Jason want? I think he should choose."

"Jason?" Gram turned toward him. "Maddy thinks it's your decision."

Jason shrugged his shoulders. Maddy suddenly felt sorry for him. Not only did he not know her position in the house, he also felt very uncomfortable being "trapped" with someone he detested. *It's as uncomfortable for him as it is for me! Actually, more so. This isn't his house at all.*

"I love scalloped," Maddy clamped her mouth shut. She had almost said "Gram" at the end of her sentence.

"If you don't mind, Jason, scalloped it is."

"Fine," he said quietly.

"What would you like me to do?" Maddy asked.

"Get an apron around that tiny waist for the first thing," Gram said. "Then I think I'll put you in charge of making green bean casserole. Here's the stuff. Here's the recipe."

After the table was set and the casseroles were in the oven, Gram made everyone go to their rooms to rest before they ate.

Maddy lay on her bed only for a moment. Then she moved to the window seat and curled up with the largest of the teddy bears on her lap. She rested her head on his and looked out into the peaceful gardens. The grass shifted colors with every break in the clouds. The flowers seemed to brighten the place, sunshine or no sunshine. Maybe that's why Gram put them there.

Maddy hated to think it, but it was awfully nice to see Jason in a place where he wasn't comfortable. This wasn't his turf, and it softened him considerably. She felt herself relaxing more and more, knowing that in front of an elderly hostess Jason would treat her with a little more consideration.

After a while, a light rap on her door let Maddy know it was time for her to dress and go to dinner.

After putting on a clean skirt and top, Maddy brushed her hair and fluffed it with her fingers. She moved down the stairs, wishing she wore something that swooped around her. The thought startled her. Conventional? Pretty? Elegant? Her? She laughed, sat on the banister and swooped down the stairs in a different way.

Downstairs, she found Gram bustling between the kitchen and dining room, placing steaming casseroles upon thick pads on her table. The small turkey was placed at the head of the table. Maddy took the chair with its back to the kitchen so she could help Gram if she needed anything. Jason sat across from Maddy.

Gram hadn't left anything out. She had set the table with a linen cloth that had a shiny, scroll pattern woven into its threads. Carefully polished silverware flanked china plates with a heavy floral pattern around the lipped edges. Maddy took her peach linen napkin from a fluted glass and placed it in her lap.

Jason did the same. He looked different with his hair newly

slicked, wearing a white shirt and narrow black tie. Maddy wanted to laugh and admire him in the same breath.

"Will you say grace, Jason?" Gram asked.

Jason stood, put his hands behind his back, and bowed his head.

Gram cleared her throat. "It isn't necessary to stand, young man."

Jason nodded and sat down. Maddy couldn't tell if he was embarrassed or if he was just uncomfortable praying in a less formal position.

"Holy Father," Jason began. "We offer you our fullest gratitude for that which you have placed before us. Amen."

Maddy blinked. Her prayers didn't sound like that. Her prayer might have been, "Hey, God, thanks for this great stuff to eat and for Gram and for some days off school." Was she praying all wrong? Maybe God never heard her prayers.

"Tell us about your family, Jason." Gram carved without standing. Loose skin from her upper arms jiggled as she tackled the turkey.

Jason told the basics, explaining that his dad and mom worked the family furniture store—one of six family-owned stores in Minnesota.

Maddy took a bite of turkey wing and raised her eyebrows. "Furniture? I thought your family were farmers."

Jason didn't answer right away. Maddy knew he thought she made fun of him. "No. Everyone is roped into taking part of the business, though."

Gram chuckled. Maddy smiled. As he kept talking, Maddy discovered he came from a small town. Maddy had never been in a small town that she could remember. Her family had driven through a few on their way to somewhere big, but they didn't stop long enough to do anything but gas up, eat, and take a bathroom break.

Jason talked of his church background in much the same way he spoke to Maddy. "The kids aren't serious about anything," he said in response to Gram's question about his cynicism toward his youth group. "They claim to be Christians, yet they talk behind each other's backs."

As Jason listed off more offenses, things began to make sense to Maddy. His overblown reactions to her. His judgments. They seemed to be rooted in his own youth group.

Perfect scalloped potatoes went into Maddy's mouth. "Was anyone as committed to God as you are?"

"Only a few. We often felt discouraged that the other kids claimed to know Christ, yet had more interest in spending time with a boyfriend or girlfriend than in learning about God. Their claims to Christianity were so fake."

Jason took a drink of sparkling cider, then turned to Gram. "I'm sorry I'm so opinionated on this, ma'am. It's just that I'm tired of non-Christians turning away from God because of phony look-alikes."

"Young man, all opinions kindly stated are welcome in my home," she reassured him.

Maddy didn't want to hear any opinions stated by Jason. "What do you do for fun?" she asked, almost picturing him spending all his time with his nose in the Bible, or prowling for offenders. She almost dropped her fork when she discovered he had backpacked to Europe, Nepal, and Africa. Equally astounding was his major—music.

"You are quite a different person than I would have guessed in a multiple–choice quiz," Maddy said.

"Now Maddy," Gram said sternly. "You can't go around judging people by how they look.…"

"Or by what they wear?" Maddy asked in false innocence.

"Of course not by what they wear," Gram said, indignant.

Jason looked anxious to change the subject. "What about your family, Maddy? Why don't you tell us about them and why you're here?" He devoured a healthy-sized piece of white meat, covered with gravy.

"I don't think that's necessary," Gram said, looking uncomfortable. "She doesn't know where they are, and it's a painful topic I do not wish to have discussed over my Thanksgiving dinner."

Now it was time for Jason to raise his eyebrows. Maddy felt something under the table, like Jason had nudged her with his foot. She looked up. Jason's eyes were begging her for an explanation. She just smiled and ate another bite. She could tell he was more than a little bit confused about how Gram would know this information. She only hoped he believed Gram had gotten the info from a phone conversation inviting her to dinner, or at some moment when he wasn't around.

"Do you miss your family?" Gram asked Jason.

Jason swallowed so hard, Maddy would've been able to see it from across the room. "Yes, ma'am. It's different than being on a back pack trip. I didn't miss them at all, then."

"I don't suppose you missed a family get-together while on those trips."

"No, ma'am."

Maddy didn't want to think about her family. "We never really had a homemade Thanksgiving dinner." When she looked up, she realized she had spoken out loud. Gram looked into her teacup. Jason looked at her.

"My parents were so busy working and all," Maddy quickly explained, "my mom just bought something pre-made. Depending on where we were and how well Dad had done, we might even go to a restaurant for dinner."

Maddy looked at Jason, and he didn't turn away. "You're lucky, you know. To have a family and memories like that to miss." She turned to her grandmother who sat next to her and kissed her on the cheek. "Thanks for the best Thanksgiving I've ever had."

Gram put her hand on Maddy's knee. "I wish it were one of many, dear."

Jason looked at them oddly again.

"Well!" Maddy said brightly, "One thing I can say about our Thanksgivings—they were never the same thing twice."

"And that's good?" Jason asked. "Knowing what to expect and what to anticipate is what made our Thanksgivings so special. Knowing how everyone would act. Who would sit where. Who would watch the bowl games and who would ignore them. What the menu would be, who would be there, and who would help out in the kitchen. Memories from one year built on the memories of another."

Like the high school parties, Maddy thought. *Were they my family?*

"What about you, Mrs. MacDonald?" Jason asked. He

glanced around the room, apparently looking for family photos. "Where did you meet your husband?"

Gram looked surprised at the question. She giggled and winked at Jason. "It's sort of a tawdry story."

"Then you don't have to tell," Jason said.

"Please do!" Maddy said eagerly.

Gram looked thoughtful. "I was a young girl, anxious to find a good man to marry. I wasn't certain where to find one. I asked my girlfriends where such a gent might be. I found this tavern downtown that served Irish coffee as well as Irish whiskey. I marched in, sat at a table, and ordered corned beef. When a young gent named MacDonald asked if he could join me, I eagerly said yes. And when he found out I was a single mother with a young son, he didn't bat an eye. 'Ask me if it matters,' he said. From that moment, I knew he was my man."

Maddy's jaw dropped open. "Grandmother!" she said without thinking.

Jason choked, almost spilling his coffee into his lap and onto the floor.

10

Maddy clapped her hand over her mouth.

Jason's eyes grew larger. "You're...? Maddy's...?" He pointed from one to the other.

"Young man!" Gram exclaimed. "You didn't know Maddy was my granddaughter?"

He shook his head, unable to speak.

Gram looked at Maddy. "You didn't tell him?"

Maddy shrugged, sheepish. "It never came up in the conversation."

Gram's eyes moved rapidly across the floor, thinking, reflecting. "You're right. No one ever did mention it."

"Gram!" Maddy was not about to let the subject go. "No one ever told me you were a single mother. Who was Dad's father? What happened?"

"Not now. We have a guest."

Jason muttered throughout their conversation. "I can't believe you didn't tell me...I mean that I didn't know...how could I have been so stupid?"

Maddy ignored him. "But this is my family. I want to know," she demanded of her grandmother.

"Another time, Maddy," Gram insisted.

Then there was silence. Only the ticking of the grandfather clock could be heard.

The phone rang, startling them all.

"Oh, my. I wonder who that could be. No one ever calls me on Thanksgiving." Gram stood and straightened her dress. She disappeared from sight and returned moments later, one eyebrow raised over dancing eyes. "It's for you, Maddy. Someone named Kick?"

Maddy felt at once surprised and disappointed, having wondered if it might be her family.

"Happy Thanksgiving!" she said into the receiver.

"You stole my line!" Kick said. "Now what am I supposed to say?"

"This is a nice surprise," Maddy said softly.

"I was bored. My family is far too plain white bread America. You were the only one I could think of calling."

"I'm glad you did."

They chatted for a couple more minutes about nothing in particular. It seemed odd to be dating, yet have nothing much to say. "Well…Happy Thanksgiving," she said again. "I guess I'd better go."

"Abandoning me, are you?"

"Like a turkey carcass," Maddy teased.

"I'd make great soup then."

"You go do that," Maddy said, laughing. "I should get back to my Gram. Hopefully your boredom won't last forever."

"Nope. Parties all weekend. I just have to survive today."

They said their good-byes and Maddy returned to the table.

"Will you tell me the story now, Gram?"

Gram shook her head and began collecting empty dishes. "I'm sorry. Our young guest here took me back to the day that held the best surprise for me. I spoke without discernment. Let's clean up." She turned to Jason. "Part of Maddy's training in the real world is that she must have some sort of pop culture education. Can you believe that she has no clue who the Brady Bunch is?"

Jason's mouth tugged into a little smile. "Impossible."

"Living the life she did allowed little television. No reruns. No junk to her brain. And no *Wizard of Oz*."

He shook his head, unbelieving.

Maddy nodded. "We never owned a TV. We moved so much, and my parents worked so hard, they figured TV was a foolish luxury."

Jason stared at her. "Didn't you watch at friends' houses?"

"We didn't have lots of friends. Besides, we got so used to entertaining ourselves without TV that when we did have the chance, we didn't watch it much."

"Wow," Jason said. "We filled up on TV until Mom kicked us out to go do other things."

"I saw movies in the theater," Maddy protested. "Not many, but some."

"You are in Seattle to get an education," Gram said firmly. "Follow me."

Maddy obeyed. Jason trailed along behind.

"And part of that education is for you to have a taste of the classics."

"Dad said television and movies are a waste of time."

"Bah," Gram said, disgusted. "Your father is an old biddy before his time. He was born an old biddy."

She led them to a small room at the back of the house. A corner sofa filled with plump cushions took up one corner, a television wall unit the other. Gram passed out afghans she had crocheted herself over the years. Maddy slipped out of her shoes and tucked her feet underneath her. Jason sat stiffly on a far end of the sofa. Then Gram popped in a video, and the movie began.

After a few minutes, Jason suddenly moaned and put his head in his hands. At first Maddy thought he was upset that the crabby old lady was taking Dorothy's dog to the pound. Then, the music started. Maddy sat upright. "Wait a minute!" She turned and stared at Jason, then back at the TV. "That's the tune you always hum when you see me!" She turned back to Elmyra Gulch on her rickety old bicycle, pedaling furiously while wearing a dress.

"AAAHHH!" Maddy shrieked. "It's me!" She started laughing, howling. "Rewind, Gram. Rewind! I've got to see this again."

Maddy laughed even harder a second time while Jason tried to disappear into the couch. She threw a pillow at him. "You toad! You were acting like I was this crabby lady!"

Jason moaned again. "Just wait, it gets worse."

"What's going on here?" Gram demanded, putting the movie on pause. "I refuse to play one more second until you explain."

Maddy explained the accident, while Jason nodded his head.

"You did look an awful lot like Elmyra Gulch on that bike.

109

You still do," Jason said sheepishly. And then, for the first time since Maddy had known him, he laughed. Gram and Maddy joined in.

Maddy chucked another pillow at Jason when she later realized the music and character were also connected to the Wicked Witch.

The next morning, after breakfast, Gram piled both Maddy and Jason into her fifteen-year-old Lincoln Continental, which was still in perfect condition. Weaving through the streets, she made her way to the base of the Space Needle. There, she bought three tickets while Maddy joked about how tacky the amusement park was. Jason, who had withdrawn again into his quiet shell, smiled but otherwise kept silent.

At the top of the Needle, Maddy was disappointed with what she saw. Lots of low gray cloud cover. Lots of rain. She moved around the observation deck that revolved slowly, being in constant motion. Jason moved at his own pace. Gram stayed in one spot, looking out across the Sound.

"I'll have to bring you on a clear day," Gram told Maddy. "Then you can see Mt. Rainier in all its splendor."

When they tired of the Needle, Gram took them on a ferry ride to Bainbridge Island, where they ate lunch at a quaint little restaurant that was actually a renovated house.

Jason and Gram seemed to get along really well. But Maddy felt like there was a barrier between she and her grandmother. A barrier of family, when the relationship should have been a gate.

Jason became the focus of Gram's attention. She asked him more about the furniture business and his part in it. She asked him about "why PCU," and why so far from home, and what kind of canoe trips he took in the boundary waters of Minnesota. Maddy felt left out. She felt like dropping way back as they walked on the island, wondering if they would even notice she wasn't there.

On the short ferry ride back to Seattle, Maddy stood in the bow behind the Lucite wind guard, watching the skyline grow larger and closer. It was a beautiful trip. But it held no emotion for her.

On Saturday, Maddy spent a lot of time in her room studying. She didn't really want to study, but she didn't want to feel alone in a group, either.

Jason left Saturday after dinner. Maddy wanted to go too, but had no excuse for leaving before Sunday afternoon. She attended church with her grandmother in the morning, ate a quiet—almost silent—lunch, then packed her bike for the trip back to the university.

"Will I see you before Christmas?" Gram asked as Maddy settled herself onto the bicycle seat.

Maddy looked at the ground. "I don't think so."

"I'll miss you," Gram said, sounding obligated.

Maddy took a deep breath. Her heart picked up speed. "You hardly talked to me," Maddy said quietly. "You talked to Jason."

"I was not comfortable with your questions." Gram said curtly. "I don't like to talk about my son."

"You don't have to talk about him," Maddy said. "You can talk about you. Or Grandfather. Or Seattle."

Gram looked uncomfortable. She wrung her hands. "I suppose…." She hesitated. "Can we try again?"

"We'll have to, won't we?" Maddy said rudely. She pedaled down the driveway without looking back, realizing too late that her abrupt departure probably had torn down the few building blocks that had been so precariously laid.

The next day, school began with a blast of information and activity, making Maddy wonder at the wisdom of taking any days off at all.

At lunch, Maddy loaded her tray, feeling back in touch with all she needed to do.

"My darling! My love!"

Maddy was smiling even before she turned toward the voice. As she did, Kick came sliding across the linoleum floor on his knees. "I have missed you deeply."

"And I you, dear sir." Maddy bowed her head, and placed her hand on his shoulder as if bestowing an honor.

Kick jumped up and looked at her, cocking his head. He put his right hand to his chin and leaned into it, supporting his right elbow with his left hand. "Something is askew here. Something is different."

Maddy shifted her weight from one foot to another.

"Hold still," Kick said as he moved around Maddy, examining her.

"I'm in the way, Kick."

"They can go around."

Maddy stood another moment, until the bottleneck of students began to glare at her. "Sorry," she apologized. To Kick she said, "I'm going now."

"No. Wait."

"Bye." Maddy walked briskly to a nearby table and sat. She picked up her fork and began to eat.

Kick came over, looked at her lunch and smacked his head. "Oh, no! Fat globules everywhere!"

Maddy smiled and smacked her lips. "And they are so, so yummy."

Kick yanked on the chair next to her. "Yummy makes you fat."

"I'm not fat. I don't intend to get fat. I'm fine. Leave me alone." Playfully she flicked a small bit of dressing toward him.

"Aack! I'm mortally wounded!" Kick said, wiping the blob off his hand with a napkin.

Maddy spoke to the other two girls at the table. "Don't mind him. He's legally insane."

Kick looked right in Maddy's face, making it difficult for her to get her fork to her mouth. "Really. What's different about you?"

"I have no clue what you're talking about."

It was an out and out lie. Maddy had left her jewelry in her room. That morning she just didn't want to put it on.

Kick tapped his fingers on the table in rapid succession, thinking. He sighed. "I'll figure it out myself if my name isn't Shakespeare Homes!"

"That's Sherlock Holmes," Maddy said. It was one of the few tidbits she remembered from junior English.

113

She waved a friend over and kept eating. After three bites, she turned toward Kick. "Hey, luv. Either get some food or get out of here. You're making me nuts."

Kick walked away, head down, scuffing his feet like a little boy.

"He's certifiable," one of the girls said. "Where'd you dig him up?"

"At a church party, if you can believe it."

"Thank you for introducing us," said the other. "We'll know where not to sit from now on."

Maddy pretended not to think twice about going to work at the library. In reality, she couldn't stop thinking about it. She didn't even feel like stopping to trace the woodwork when she got to the front doors.

Inside, Alma gave her a broad-smiled welcome. "You're on your own now, Maddy. Until you learn reference, you'll just have to check the list at the circulation desk for what needs to be done."

"Jason loves reference," Maddy said quietly. "I wouldn't want to ever take that from him."

"That's nice of you, but everyone needs to know everyone else's job. We'll wait until after the winter holidays to teach you that. Just get really good at what you know now."

Maddy nodded and went to the list. Many books had been returned that day, as well as the night before. She took a loaded cart and moved into the aisles.

She passed Jason and gave him a half-smile. He nodded his head at her, without smiling. *Without glaring, either!* A nervousness she hadn't realized she felt drained away. With a new peace, Maddy moved into the rhythm of shelving the books, looking inside the ones that especially drew her attention. She forgot time.

"Maddy. Are you going to stay here all night?"

Looking up at Jason, Maddy shook her head. She couldn't believe that he was voluntarily speaking to her!

"Just thought I'd let you know it's five-thirty."

With that, Jason left.

Maddy stood there for a long time, just thinking about this unexpected turn of events.

11

Maddy strode through the green, her boots glistening with leftover rain. As she wandered·into the grove, Kick slid out from behind a tree and reached for her hand. "Come here."

Maddy giggled. "Kick!"

Kick pulled her into a stand of cedar trees that grew close enough together to form a hide-out. He sat on a piece of plastic, with his back to one of the trees, and pulled Maddy down to sit beside him. "I had a great Thanksgiving."

Maddy rolled her eyes. "First you call and tell me how bored you are. Then you come back to school and say it was great. And now you ask me to meet you out here so you can tell me something I already heard?"

"I didn't finish the story. I had a great Thanksgiving because there were so many great parties."

Maddy's eyes narrowed. "You didn't meet anyone new, did you?"

"No, ma'am. I met some new stuff." His hand disappeared into his leather jacket and returned clenching something.

Slowly he opened his fist. As he did, his face and eyes grew bright with anticipation.

"It's a joint. So?" Maddy glanced around quickly to make certain their spot could not be seen by anyone walking by. "You've had hundreds of joints." She tried to sound nonchalant, when in reality her heart had started beating faster.

"This one is different stuff. It's better. The high is incredible. And I wanted my girl to be the first to share it with me." He grinned widely. Before she could respond, he had the joint lit. He drew in deeply and looked at her with heavy lidded eyes. Then, with a look of one bestowing a fabulous gift, he handed her the joint.

Maddy bit her bottom lip. She wanted to so badly. Yet something had changed inside her. Now her desire to do this one thing God's way weighed stronger in her mind. As she quietly observed her own new choices, Kick took the joint from her and took another long drag.

He sat in silence, wrapped up in the warm, heady flavor. A moment after he exhaled, he looked at her. "You aren't getting to be straight, are you?"

He took another toke and offered it to her, as if giving her a chance to prove she wasn't.

Maddy put her hand up. "You can think what you want of me, Kick. But I'm not going to do something wrong for anyone, no matter how good it feels."

Kick looked at her through narrowed eyes. "You're telling me this is wrong?" he held the joint up, examining it carefully. He slowly shook his head. "No, Maddy. This is very good."

"Yeah, it is," Maddy agreed. "But it's still wrong, isn't it? It's illegal. It can cause brain damage…." she wanted to say more, but even she had to admit her arguments sounded weak. She couldn't explain what she knew to be true in her heart. She tried a tactic she hoped would get through to Kick.

"I'm worried about your grades." The more she talked, the more uncomfortable she felt. She wanted to leave; yet she wanted to stay and talk some sense into Kick. She adored him, and understood the joy and necessity of living for parties. She wanted to stay and fall under the wonderful spell of marijuana. "Kick, you're going to ruin your grades."

"No, I won't. I've got it all under control." He watched the smoke curl up into the trees.

"Kick…."

He waved her off. "Go. Go away. I don't want to talk to you. I don't want to see you until you've got some more sense in you."

Maddy stood, but didn't go.

"I said, *leave.*"

Maddy walked quickly out of the grove and into the rainy afternoon. All the way to the library she thought about how frustrated she was with Kick. How much she wanted to do things the right way, but how hard that was. Then she wondered why she even bothered with Kick. Finally, she decided she could see herself in Kick. If she abandoned him, she would feel like she was turning on herself.

Maddy checked the task list and went to the back room to bind magazines. There, Maddy picked up a stack and put them in the clamp, wondering if she could remember all the steps correctly. With the effort of putting her whole body into sawing slits into the bindings, she never heard Jason come in the room. She didn't realize he was there until he was very close.

"You smell funny," Jason said, sniffing the air like a blood-hound.

"You look funny," Maddy said unkindly, without looking up from her work.

"I thought you didn't...." Jason's voice trailed off.

Maddy stopped then and looked at him. She held the saw aloft. "I didn't what?"

Jason's eyes narrowed. He breathed deeply. "Are you doing okay?"

Maddy put the saw back to the magazines. "Having a bad day. You'll survive better if you leave me alone."

"Done." Jason backed out of the room and closed the door.

Maddy felt in a blue funk the rest of the week. Every time she looked, Kick was either high, or on the way down. Jason seemed to be snooping into her business. He always seemed to be there, listening to her conversations with Kick and scowling.

Sarah's new clothing was adorable, but Maddy hated the guys who now constantly swarmed around her roommate—insecure, immature, shallow types who drooled over Sarah's every move. It irritated Maddy that Sarah grew wide-eyed and silent, hardly responding to the hordes. Her breathy, shy, "hi," seemed to make the guys all the more crazy for her. Maddy would have said something if she was in a better mood.

Each night Maddy read the Psalms, but even those seemed depressing. It seemed like her prayers went as far as the wall—

not even making it as far as the ceiling.

On Saturday she waltzed into The Cup & Chaucer with the fragile hope that her work would bring her some happiness.

Brad scowled at her. "Joe Plimco came by. He's bringing more snacks, like you asked."

"What's wrong with that? That's great!" Maddy felt better already.

"He thought it was such a great idea, he's thinking of making this a sandwich shop, too."

"Oh."

"That means more workers. More health and sanitation people coming in to inspect. More people who have food on their minds, rather than rest and intelligent conversation. More jokers who will make fun of our poets, story readers, and musicians. I don't like this, Maddy. It's not right. I'll have to find a new job."

"No! What would I do without you?"

Brad gave her a hard look. "Run the place."

Maddy turned away. She found a rag and started dusting where she had left off the week before. It seemed that all the problems in her little world were her fault. She'd snapped at Sarah again and hurt her feelings. Kick was unhappy with her. Nothing was going right.

Maddy threw herself into her work. After awhile, she even found a small measure of the peace she'd sought. She was glad when the place filled with people and coffee. She was glad to get the messiness of life out of her mind.

"Where's my woman?"

Maddy, serving coffee in the rear of the room, cringed at the sound. "Tell me I didn't just hear that," she said to the customers.

"I want my woman!" came the demand from the front of the shop.

"'Fraid you did," the middle-aged man said. "You know him?"

"Hmm. A little too well, I'm sorry to say."

The man's wife spoke. "I'm told they mellow out after fifty. Before then, it's a lost cause." She leaned over, giving her husband a playful peck on the cheek.

"Thanks for the advice," Maddy said. She wanted to avoid Kick. Not now. Not here.

"Oh W-o-m-a-n! Where a-r-e you?"

Maddy longed for some sort of trap door that would open up beneath her feet. Or perhaps a moving panel of books. Maybe just a paper bag over her head would do the trick.

"Ahh, there she is! The light of my life! The beauty of the world."

Kick trotted over to her on tippy-toes. "Come with me, my love. And we shall be away from this drudgery!" He held her hand over his head, trotting again on tippy-toes. Maddy could do nothing but trail behind him with an apologetic look on her face. A light applause followed her across the room.

"I'm going to die of embarrassment, Kick."

"Not you! You love life and all the fun it brings."

"I don't like an audience."

Brad leaned across the bar, wiping a glass clean. "And I don't like a show in my coffee house."

Kick returned his stern look. "And I don't like bossy bosses."

"Can I try and talk some sense into him?" Maddy asked Brad.

"Please do. But out back."

Kick followed Maddy through the bowels of the store and out the back door.

"Good. Gives me a chance to try to win you over once again."

"You haven't lost me, Kick."

He put his hand inside his coat. Maddy closed her eyes, willing for it not to be a replay of earlier in the week. "Kick, please don't."

"Oh, Maddy," Kick said in a swooning voice, "Please do." He lit up.

Maddy decided to take a less motherly approach. She beamed a huge smile at him. "Want to make me happy?"

She heard a sound beyond him and looked around the dumpster to the mouth of the alley, just twenty feet away, expecting to see her homeless friends. Instead, Jason was walking by with one of his buddies. Kick leaned around the dumpster and said, "Hey, wanna join our party? We've got some killer stuff here."

Jason looked at Maddy for what seemed like a forever moment. He stared hard. She could almost hear his silent accusations. Her face flaming, Maddy shoved Kick out of Jason's view. Jason walked away without a word.

"Now look what you've done! You are going to destroy me, Kick." Maddy said, trying to restrain the explosive anger in her voice.

"Never in a million. I'm trying to get you hooked up with the best, and you won't listen," Kick pouted.

"I'm going back to work."

"I'll come inside in a moment."

"Please don't."

"You're telling me no again?" His pout deepened.

Maddy opened the screen and pushed open the solid door. "Yes. I am telling you no."

She stomped inside and reached the bar just as Jason and his buddy walked in. "Party over?" Jason asked dryly.

"There never was a party," Maddy said through clenched teeth.

"Didn't look like that to me," Jason countered.

Maddy reluctantly took their order and served them. The whole time, Brad leaned against the rear counter. He watched Maddy, never taking his eyes off her. After Jason and his friend sat down with their coffee, Brad took a long whiff of the air around her. "An interesting aroma you brought back with you, Maddy."

"Sorry. It's not my fault," she said flatly. She grabbed the broom, sweeping fallen coffee beans into a small pile.

"If you're going to do something stupid, the rule is to do it on your own time," Brad warned.

Maddy grabbed the dust pan. With every movement she slammed things around. "I'm not doing anything stupid."

Brad shrugged. "See it your way. From my point of view, it's stupid. A waste of time, money, and brain cells."

Maddy swung around. "Look. I'm trying to keep Kick from doing something stupid. I'm not a party girl any more. Sure it's tough for me to say no. I've had plenty of good times to reflect on. But it's not happening right now, okay?"

Brad leaned on his hands. "Be careful, Maddy."

Maddy took a deep breath and went to the restroom where she sprayed Lysol into the air and stood underneath the droplet shower. She did it a second time until she felt like she would choke. As she yanked open the door, she wished she had her bracelets on. The jangle would have given her a tiny bit of comfort.

She burst into the front of the shop and swooped down on the tables, collecting empties and asking about refills. "How about a smile, Maddy?" someone called to her.

"I lost it last week," she muttered.

She cut the corner around the bar so close, she almost lost her tray of empties.

"Slow down," Brad said.

Maddy didn't bother turning around when she heard the door jangle. She rinsed every mug and placed them all in the steaming soapy water.

"Hey!" she heard. She closed her eyes. "Tell me it isn't true," she said to Brad.

"Loverboy is back. And he's helping himself to a chair at the table of that guy you just served."

Maddy dropped her head forward, leaning it on the cabinet. "Not Jason."

"Yeah. That's the dude. Do you want to know what he's doing?"

"No. Yes. No. Do I want to?"

"Probably not." Brad was good at pretending he was working when, in reality, he was watching everything that was going on. "Loverboy is talking."

"I can hear him."

They both listened.

"You got a problem with my girlfriend?" Kick asked Jason. "I've heard you treat her bad."

"No worse than you," Jason said quietly.

"Hey! I treat my woman the way she should be treated. You gotta sweet talk 'em and then set 'em straight."

Maddy felt weak.

"I just feel like resting here. Mind?"

"Yes," Jason said in his quiet way. "We had an important conversation going."

"I'll just join in. Can I finish your cookie?" Kick asked Jason's friend. The friend pushed it toward him. Kick popped the whole thing in his mouth. "Great. Got any more?"

"Look…" Jason began.

Maddy imagined the whole coffee shop had their collective attention focused on table number five. Poor Jason.

"We came to this place for a quiet cup of coffee and a conversation between the two of us," Jason was saying. "If you wish to talk about the Bible, you're welcome to stay."

"That old thing?" Kick said, laughing and tipping back in the chair. "Dusty. Boring. Out of date. Next subject?"

"That is our conversation for the evening. Take it or leave it."

Brad put down the mug he'd been drying for the past five minutes. "I think it's time I make an appearance."

"Thank you," Maddy breathed.

Brad moved around the counter, a mountain with a purpose. "Hello, gentlemen," he said. "I believe I need to speak with Mr. Kick. Would you mind excusing him from your table?"

"Not at all," Jason replied.

Kick stood, his body relaxed and slow. "Call me Speedy."

Brad waited, then motioned Kick to move ahead of him. He opened the front door. "I'd like a private word, please Mr. Kick."

Kick nodded. "That's cool."

Once the door closed, Maddy could hear nothing. She could see Kick gesturing and pointing at her. Brad stood with his arms crossed. His stance made him look wider. Stronger. Finally, Kick threw up his arms and left. Brad waited a moment before he opened the door to come in again.

The instant the door opened, the conversation in the shop picked up once again, as if it had never stopped.

"Thank you," Maddy said again.

Brad shook his head. "I don't know what you see in that guy."

"He's funny. He takes me as I am."

"Does he?"

Brad stuck his hand in the hot soapy water and pulled out a mug. He plunged it into the equally steaming rinse water, then began to dry it.

Conversation over.

12

Maddy tried to avoid Kick the following day by not going to lunch in the dining room after church, although she hated spending her precious money on junk food—especially when she was alone.

At The Cup & Chaucer, she begged Brad to let her clean the bathrooms, the hallway, the outside of the building—anything if it looked like Kick was coming in. Brad looked at her, his eyebrows raised. "Sure. Scrub the toilets with a toothbrush. Fine with me."

Maddy had never been so thankful not to see someone in her entire life. She'd heard that several parties were planned for the evening and hoped that Kick had gone to one of those.

She cleaned the bathrooms, anyway. It gave her time to think and pray.

Sometimes she liked Kick. He was fun. He cared about her. He enjoyed being with her. He made her laugh. He liked her outrageous style.

"Okay, God. Let me know what you think, okay? I don't know how this works with you. But I know you're supposed to help us when we've got tough decisions. So work on this one, okay?"

Nothing happened all that night. In each class the next day, Maddy expected something. She got nothing. In the library, Jason asked if he could talk to her when their work was done. Maddy put on a very straight face as she answered. "You seem awfully serious, young man."

"It is serious, Maddy," Jason said.

"Can you give me a clue?"

"No clues. At five, I'll meet you in the binding room."

A little after five, Maddy and Jason sat down at the binding room table.

"I want to talk about Kick." Jason said.

"Sorry about the other night. He can be so funny, or he can be so obnoxious."

Jason ignored the apology. "He's no good for you, Maddy."

"You have no right to say so. You don't even know him."

"He's going to make you fall—if you haven't already."

"Like you should care! Besides, you don't think I have any place to fall from. Remember? I'm a liar about my faith because I dress funny."

"Listen. I've been watching how he treats you. He puts you down in subtle ways. I've heard him make fun of your humor, your personality, your clothes, your weight—and you aren't even close to being overweight!" Jason suddenly blushed and looked away.

"He's only joking," Maddy half-protested. She'd always

secretly wondered if he *was* joking.

Jason regained his composure. "If he's joking, how come your face gets a hurt look? And how come his voice changes to a snarl when he says it?"

"It's his way of being funny." Even to Maddy, the defense sounded weak.

"Maddy. He's a loser."

For a moment, Maddy had almost fallen for Jason's observations. But this judgment was intolerable. "You don't *know* him," Maddy said, jumping up from the table. "You, Mr. Jason Stone, the judge of all time—you need to get to know someone before you go making pronouncements on them."

"'By their fruits you shall know them,'" Jason said.

"Oh, brother. 'Bible Man' is right. So Kick doesn't have 'fruits'—whatever those are. He's not even a Christian." She could feel her voice going up the scale. "And you have these fruits?"

"I'm not going to bring myself into this argument," Jason said calmly. His eyes begged her to believe him. "It's about you. It's about Kick. And I wouldn't be here if I hadn't...well, kinda gotten to know your heart a little."

Maddy leaned across the table, her anger dissipated by surprise. Her voice was calm. "*He's* got a good heart, too. It's just getting buried under some bad decisions. But he can pull out of it. He will."

"You're certain of this." Jason looked at her, locking in with her gaze.

"I was there, Jason. Before I became a Christian I went to every party I possibly could. I've tried most of the common drugs—cocaine, ecstasy, marijuana, ludes. I've drunk enough to know what my limit is, what I like, and what I don't like. I've been there. I came out. It doesn't have to be a permanent state of existence."

"And you think you're the one who can pull him out of this." Jason's brows raised. A smirk tugged at the corners of his mouth.

"Obviously, you don't think so."

Jason shook his head slowly. "No. I don't."

"Thanks for the vote of confidence." Maddy felt like sticking her tongue out at him.

"You're too close to him, Maddy. You're too close to the party scene yourself. One bad day and you'll be back there, too."

Maddy had to admit it, Jason's face registered honest concern. Almost like she had imagined a big brother might act.

"I've been tested, and I made it," Maddy blurted.

Jason raised his eyebrow. He put his hand through his hair and leaned back in his chair. "You can't put an ex-drinker into a bar and expect them to save everyone there. You've got to have some years and growth between you and your experiences first before you can go around saving people from the same situation."

"I don't have years to wait," Maddy protested. Her eyes pleaded with him to understand. "Kick is here now. He needs help now. He needs me now."

Jason threw up his hands. "I disagree. I think he's pulling you down. I think he's treating you pretty lousy. If you were my sister, I'd have punched him out by now."

"Hmmm," Maddy said, amused. "That's almost word for word what Kick said about you and how you treated me."

Jason got flustered, dropping the chair to its four feet. He stood. "Well, that was different. The Bible and God are my first responsibility. Do what you want about Kick. For a moment I forgot you weren't my sister." Jason left the room abruptly.

From her sitting position, Maddy stretched her legs out and twirled her feet at the ankles. She put her chin in her hands and sat there a long time. Thinking. Pondering. Amazed. *Sister?*

In a daze, she went home to grab Sarah for dinner.

"What do you think, Sarah?" Maddy asked, buttoning her blouse. "Is Kick a jerk?"

"No. I don't think he's a *jerk*." Sarah didn't look at Maddy. She fiddled with her hair while staring in the mirror.

Maddy looked at her roommate carefully. "But you're not thinking lots of positive things about him."

Sarah waited a moment, then shook her head slowly.

"What is it?" Maddy demanded.

They continued to talk as they walked toward the dining hall.

Sarah smiled to herself, remembering. "He used to make me laugh."

"And still does."

"Sure," Sarah said, tucking her hair behind her ear. "But now he makes fun of you a lot. He wants me to laugh at you." She looked around at the students from all over campus, converging at the dining hall. "He acts like you're some idiot female who's lost in the Dark Ages."

Maddy burst into a laugh. "Me? In the Dark Ages?"

"He ridicules what you do, what you wear, how you talk. It's almost as if he really doesn't like you, but you're so much fun to pick at he stays with you."

Maddy swallowed. She got into the line that snaked down the hall into the Student Union Building, or SUB as the students called it. "Do you think he doesn't like me?"

"Oh, no!" Sarah said quickly. "Maybe it's that he likes you, but is one of those people who doesn't know how to show it. They do real stupid things and doesn't even realize they are hurting someone. Does that make sense?"

"Sort of."

Two guys behind them started talking to Sarah. Maddy was too much into her own little world to notice or care. Moments later, Kick walked up and put his arms around her waist. "How's my one and only?" he asked, then nibbled her ear.

"Thinking," Maddy said absently.

"About what?" he whispered in her ear.

"You," Maddy said honestly.

Kick let go and spun around in a circle. "She's thinking about me! Yippee."

"Can we talk somewhere tonight?" Maddy asked. She took a tray, then handed Kick one.

"Sure. Where?"

"The Sub," Maddy said. "Or downstairs in the Pizza Den."

Maddy usually ate her biggest meal at dinner. Tonight she didn't put much on her tray and only nibbled what she had.

"You're going to waste away into nothingness," Kick said, shoveling huge forks of mashed potatoes into his mouth.

Maddy put her fork down and looked at him. "Which is it,

132

Kick? Am I going to waste away or become the fattest lady?"

"Both!" he said, holding his fork aloft. His grin irritated her.

Maddy nodded. "I'm going to my room for something. I'll be downstairs by eight. Okay?"

"See you baby! Give me a kiss." Kick puckered his lips way out and Maddy planted a half-hearted kiss in return. When she stood, she caught Jason turning away.

She asked Sarah to stay lost until eight, mentioning she needed time alone. Sarah didn't seem to care. She was more wrapped up in her new male friends.

In her room, Maddy took out her Bible. She turned page by page until she reached the presentation page. She ran her fingers over the words and then turned to the Psalms. She didn't know what she expected to find. She didn't really think she'd find anything. She just wanted to be with God and ask him some questions.

She almost didn't need to. Her heart told her what was right. Peace in spite of pain confirmed it.

Just before eight, she walked mechanically out the door.

In the SUB, Maddy found Kick playing a wild and vocal Foosball game with some other guy she recognized as Eric. Everyone called him Eric the Red because of his bright red hair. He had the reputation for being a wild guy. Maddy sat on a vinyl sofa and waited.

"Cheer for me, baby," Kick shouted. "I need a cheerleader. Get up. Wave those pom-poms."

Normally, Maddy would have laughed. Her laughing mechanism had shut down days ago. She tried to smile. She sat cross-legged and watched the two battle it out as if huge sums of money were involved. Eric won and gloated over it.

"Tomorrow night!" Kick said. "The winner gets the best rolled stuff in town."

"That's what you promised me tonight," Eric said. "Pay up."

"If I pay up, it will be gone tomorrow," Kick said.

"And if you don't pay up, it will be gone tomorrow."

"Pig." Kick reached into his coat.

"Loser." Eric said with a huge grin. "Next time we play for her," he said.

Maddy knew he was teasing. But in her mood it wasn't funny.

"Deal!" Kick said with far too much enthusiasm.

Eric sauntered away, shouting hellos, good-byes, and slapping high-fives with others as he left the large room.

Kick flopped onto the sofa and put his arm around Maddy. "Sorry, babe. I know I've disappointed you. I'll win next time."

"Kick. There won't be a next time." Maddy felt stupid, her words awkward.

He cocked his head. This wasn't going very well. "I mean," Maddy said, "I think we should break up."

"Break up? Break up?" He flipped his arm off her shoulder and stared at her. "I didn't even know we were going together." He looked her up and down as if quite offended.

Maddy touched his arm, her eyes shouting while her voice remained calm. "Don't try to be funny. This is serious."

"I am serious." He pulled his face into the exaggerated look of a very serious person.

"Kick. We're done seeing each other." She rubbed his arm, hoping the touch would make it easier for him to accept.

"Nah-ah. We have a lot more days, and nights, and kisses, and fun times ahead," Kick said, counting off on his fingers. He threw his hands in the air. "We're not done. Why, we're not even half-baked!"

Maddy slapped her hands on her knees. "Look, I mean business."

"Oh, now we're just ending our business relationship. Cool. I always wanted it to be personal." His head bounced, his lips pursed in thought.

Maddy looked at Kick. "You know exactly what I'm trying to say, don't you?"

"Of course I do." He nodded wildly, a broad grin dominating his expression. "You love me and want to spend tonight and the rest of your life with me."

"It's not good...."

"I know. Hey! Isn't that a verse from your Bible or something? I like that one. It's not good for man to be lonely, or something like that."

Maddy clenched her lips together. "I'm leaving this room. And when I leave— "

"You want me to follow you everywhere you go." Kick didn't look at her. His eyes had a dull pained look to them.

"—I will no longer be your girl, your woman, or any other title that insinuates or announces that we are in a relationship." The words came easily. In spite of the pain, she knew she was doing the right thing. "I do not want to see you or eat meals with you or have you come into The Cup & Chaucer. I wish I could be your friend, but I don't know if we could be friends, either."

"It's that Jason guy, isn't it? You're in love with him," Kick said, his accusation weak.

Maddy stood. "Thanks for the laughs, Kick." She walked away before he could see the tears streaming down her face.

Back in her room, she went straight to bed and put her face in the pillow. She tried to cry quietly, but that didn't work. Sarah came over and rubbed her back. Maddy wanted Sarah to go away and leave her alone, but then she would have to talk to her and tell her that. So she endured and tried to ignore the hand attempting to comfort her.

Eventually, the tears subsided and a deep sleep came.

13

Maddy moved through the week in slow motion. She found herself looking for Kick, then hating what she saw when she did locate him. He never once tried to call, speak to her, or sit with her. Even though that's what Maddy told him to do, it still hurt her.

She avoided Jason, who wore a glum, almost angry expression all week. In her spare time, she applied herself more to her studies, taking her books to the library and curling up in one of the library's cushioned chairs. If Maddy left dinner early, she could sit reading her books for three hours before the library closed.

The more she spent time in the library, the more words seemed to be flowing through her blood. The more she touched the front doors and walked through them, the more they were like open arms welcoming her home. She secretly wished she could bring a blanket and pillow, and cradle herself to sleep amidst the millions of words.

On Thursday afternoon, Maddy walked into the suite, where she found Sarah sitting on the sofa, talking on the phone.

"Oh, wait," Sarah said into the phone. "She just walked in." Sarah held the phone out. "It's Brad."

"What are you calling for?" Maddy asked.

"That's a nice greeting," Brad said.

"Sorry. I'm not used to talking to you on the phone."

"There's a first time for everything," Brad said brightly.

"True enough."

"Then will it be the first time Ms. Maddy MacDonald has worked at The Cup & Chaucer on a Thursday night?" He sounded more than hopeful, like he was begging.

Maddy mentally reviewed her schedule. "Which Thursday?"

"This one. Today."

"What time?"

"Now."

"Planning ahead are we?" Maddy asked.

"Cute. Joe Plimco just called. He doesn't plan ahead. He asked a bunch of his buddies over for coffee, munchies, dessert, and a little music. The caterers will be here any minute with the food."

"Just so long as I'm not the music," Maddy teased.

Brad laughed. "How soon can you be here?"

Maddy looked in the mirror to be sure her clothes weren't wrinkled or dirty. "I'm on my way."

The evening passed quickly. Joe's friends were as loud and boisterous as he was. The hired bluegrass trio had the guests howling, clapping, and stomping their feet. Parties Tonight Catering provided a small buffet of buffalo wings, carrots, celery sticks, broccoli, and bell peppers. A tray of potato skins and deep fried mozzarella cheese sticks were kept warm on a hot tray. Joe had Maddy put bowls of ranch dressing and stacks of napkins on every table.

Every few minutes, Maddy moved through the tables picking up soiled napkins and empties. She memorized what type of coffee each person drank and kept a full hot mug in front of him at all times. That part wasn't too bad. Most of these guys liked their coffee redneck. No sissy lattés. They thought cappuccinos were wimpy because they came in demitasse cups and had froth on top.

A few faces peered in through the plate glass windows after looking at the closed sign on the door. A handful knocked, hoping to be let in anyway.

"I told you we should put a 'Private Party' sign on the door," Maddy told Brad.

"The boss was fine with what we had."

At ten, the music ended. Some of the men took their overcoats and were gone minutes after saying a "thank you" to the host. Others milled around, slapping each other on the back, laughing.

"Why didn't they invite their wives? Their girlfriends?" Maddy muttered as she returned to the bar with a load of dirty dishes.

"You don't know what this is?" Brad asked.

"Joe's buddies."

"Every month they have a boys' night out. Each one of these businessmen plans some sort of fun, clean entertainment so they can get together and enjoy their friendship."

"I hate it when men exclude their wives."

"Everyone needs time alone with same-gender friends. Men have gotten a bad rep because some have done pretty stupid things. These guys are great. They have fun. Male friendships build stronger marriages."

"Okay, okay."

As Maddy wove in and out of the remaining clusters of talking men, she eavesdropped and decided that perhaps they were pretty harmless, after all.

When she returned to the counter, Brad started talking without looking up from his cleaning. "I haven't seen the face of that bozo boyfriend of yours plastered against the window this evening. What happened? Didn't you tell him where you were going?"

"No, I didn't tell him. He's not my boyfriend any more."

Brad stopped scouring the inside of the espresso machine. He stared at Maddy. "Whoa. What happened?"

Maddy willed the tears not to pool up in her eyes. "Someone opened the refrigerator door and the light came on."

Brad nodded. "Illumination is a good thing for the soul."

Maddy ventured into the room with a washrag. Joe Plimco grabbed her by the arm. "Did a great job tonight." He held out a wad of bills. "The guys gave these to me. It's your tip."

Maddy pushed it away. "This is my job, Mr. Plimco."

He tucked the bills into her apron pocket. "Keep it. They're generous when they've had a good time. You helped make it that way."

"Brad did, too," Maddy said.

"Don't worry about him. He's got his own tip coming." Mr. Plimco patted his pocket.

"Thank you very much, Mr. Plimco."

Mr. Plimco clasped his hands in front of him. "It was a good move putting you here, Maddy."

"Thanks," she smiled. "I love it."

"Good."

Maddy turned to go.

"Wait," Joe called to her. "See all this leftover food? Take it to the dorm. You'll be the hit of the night."

Maddy smiled, knowing it would never reach the dorm. "Thanks, Mr. Plimco. You've just made some very special people quite happy. I'll be sure to let them know it's from you."

Joe waved her off. "Nah. No need."

Maddy dug through the cupboards to find large paper plates, then put a little of everything on each plate, making three solid meals. These she stacked and took out back.

"Mr. Duckworth, are you out here?"

A moment later, Mr. Duckworth and his friends came out of the shadows. "What are you doing here tonight, Miss Maddy?"

"Special occasion. The owner brought in lots of food and let me do with the extra what I wanted. I figured you could have an early Christmas feast."

She passed out a plate to each, then disappeared inside to get the mugs of coffee. The group sat cross-legged on the ground. The woman perched on an upended plastic milk crate.

Maddy brought out an extra mug and sat down on the ground with them, her back to the alley. She felt the crinkle of the money in her pocket. "God gave me this for you," she said, reaching into the pocket. "Use it for something you need. Toothbrushes, toothpaste, food, whatever."

It took her a moment to get all the bills together. Then she leaned forward and shoved the wad into Mr. Duckworth's lap. She put her finger to her lips and said quietly. "Please don't tell anyone."

The woman on the crate reached into her pocket and came out with a clenched fist. She leaned forward and opened Maddy's hand. Duckworth seemed to be trying to look around them into the alley. Maddy's hand closed around a small object.

"Who is that?" Duckworth called out. "What do you want?"

Maddy turned in time to see a figure moving quickly down the street. "Who was that?"

"Some kid," Duckworth said. "Seemed to be interested in our food here. He looked well-fed to me."

Maddy opened her hand. Inside was a safety pin. Attached, were two little red and white crocheted ice skates—the blades made of paper clips.

"I keep string," the woman said. "And sometimes when our clothes unravel I save the thread. I like makin' things. I thought you'd look pretty with this on."

Tears made the ice skates blurry. "It's an incredible gift," Maddy said.

"Put it on," the warbly voice insisted.

Maddy pinned the skates to her sweater.

"You're our friend," the woman said. "Most people don't think of us as human bein's. Friends give friends gifts."

"I will treasure this," Maddy said, patting her shoulder where the skates now hung.

The back door of The Cup & Chaucer opened and Brad stuck out his head. "I hate to break up this happy little feast, but I need Maddy's help closing up."

"Go, go," Duckworth said, waving a carrot stick at her.

Maddy remembered nothing of the bike ride home. It almost surprised her when her dorm appeared in front of her. She'd been too busy being happy and thanking God for little surprises.

She patiently listened to Sarah's chatter about what guys were interested in her and which ones had asked her to the Christmas party and what a terrible decision she had to make about which one to go with.

Maddy went to sleep with a smile on her face. Bad days may happen, bad weeks may get her down, but on the whole, life was going to be okay.

The next day she wore her pin. She couldn't help feeling very good about herself. She'd done something nice for some others and made them feel better in the process.

In the afternoon, she went to work at the library. The moment she opened the door, Alma hopped up from her seat. "The office rang," she said, then pursed her lips together. "The dean wants to see you right away."

Maddy's brows pulled together as thoughts quickly spun

through her mind. Finals weren't until the following week. It couldn't be her grades.

Alma wrung her hands. "Do you know what this is about?"

Maddy shook her head.

"Don't keep him waiting. I told him I would send you straightaway."

Maddy arrived at the Dean's office breathing a little harder than usual. "Hi. I'm Maddy MacDonald."

The fiftyish secretary gave her a hard look. "Mr. Brehman is expecting you."

Maddy pushed through a waist-high swinging door and followed the secretary into a large office. There, the dean sat in a royal blue swivel chair, behind a huge, highly polished wooden desk. The secretary motioned for Maddy to sit in a high-back chair with the same royal blue leather and brass rivet-puckered indents.

The dean—a tall, slender man in his late fifties—sat very still. His black suit hung on him as though he had recently lost twenty pounds. His features were sharp and well defined.

"Maddy MacDonald?" he asked.

Maddy nodded.

He wasted no time. "Your grandfather would be disgraced."

Maddy's face lost all color and she felt icy cold. "I'm sorry?" she managed to squeak.

"The activities you were involved in late last evening have been reported to this office." The dean pressed his thin lips so tightly, they seemed to disappear.

144

Thoughts spun through Maddy's mind. What had she done?

"I'm not sure I know what you mean." Maddy rubbed the leather with her thumbs.

He nodded once. "Go ahead. Tell me what happened last night."

Maddy swallowed hard. "I worked at The Cup & Chaucer. I don't usually do that on weeknights."

He nodded again. "And what happened there?"

"I served coffee to a group of men my boss is friends with." She wondered if her playful talk with the men had been taken wrong.

"What happened after that?"

Maddy blinked. "I took all the leftover food to the homeless people outside." *That's it! Maybe Mr. Plimco is mad I didn't take it to the dorm. I disobeyed him.*

Mr. Brehman leaned forward and gave her a false smile. "Yes. And then what happened?"

"My boss came out and I had to go help clean up. I did, then I rode my bike back to the dorm and went straight to bed."

"We're missing something here."

Maddy looked from side to side. What could she have forgotten? Her eyes caught framed degrees on the walls, a paned window looking out on the greens below, a tall replica of some kind of antique cabinet. "I'm sorry, sir. I'm not sure I know what I missed."

"You made a payment to one of those people who were sitting around out back," Mr. Brehman prompted.

"I gave my tip to Mr. Duckworth."

"Ahh," Mr. Brehman said, taking a pencil and writing on a notepad. "A Mr. Duckworth."

"Is it wrong for me to give my money to a homeless person?"

He leaned back in his chair. "That all depends." The chair swiveled to one side and Mr. Brehman stood. He walked around to the front of the desk and perched on one corner. From there, he looked much like a vulture, ready to devour his victim once it died. *In this case, of fright,* Maddy thought.

He leaned over and glanced at the open file on his desk.

"Isn't it true that you are here on special dispensation of the Board of Administrators of Pacific Cascades University?" He asked without looking up.

"Yes."

He read some more. "And with that special dispensation aren't there some guidelines, or rules, that must be strictly adhered to in order for you to benefit from an education from this institution?"

"Yes, sir."

Mr. Brehman sat up, looking directly at her. "List them for me, please."

"I must live on campus, participate in a work-study program, get a 3.2 grade average...."

Mr. Brehman nodded at each one. "And?"

"And no drugs." Maddy felt herself grow pasty white. She wasn't guilty, but Kick was. Did they mix her up with him? Jason was entirely right. She should have split up with him the moment she knew he was doing drugs.

Mr. Brehman nodded. He left his perch and began to pace

146

the room, hands behind his back. "So you and Mr. Duckworth had a small transaction."

"Excuse me?"

"You gave him money. And in return...."

Maddy stared at the engraved brass nameplate on the desk. After thinking, she looked up at Mr. Brehman. "Mr. Duckworth didn't give me anything in return."

"Ahh!" he said, his long skinny index finger jabbing the air. "But one of the others in the group did. This person took something from inside a pocket and gave it to you."

"Yes, that's true," Maddy said, touching her shoulder.

"And what kind of drugs were they?"

Maddy felt like she couldn't breathe. It took her a moment to get the words out. "No drugs. No. Not at all. The woman gave me these skates." She touched her shoulder again.

Mr. Brehman stopped, his mouth open as he paused in mid-speech. He moved close to Maddy and started to peer at her shoulder, then thought better of it, withdrawing quickly. He held out his hand. "May I?"

Maddy fumbled with the safety pin as if she'd only discovered them in the past twenty-four hours. Her hand shook as she placed the skates in his bony hand.

Mr. Brehman studied them carefully. "Can someone verify this?"

"The only people there were the homeless people."

Mr. Brehman resumed his pacing. "The gentleman who reported this is a reliable, upstanding citizen of this university community. Are you willing to say he lied?"

She gasped. "Sir, I am telling you the truth. As for me saying

147

someone else lied about me, I don't presume something like that. It seems to me this must be a terrible misunderstanding. It has to be. There's only one person I can think of who would—"

"Yes."

Now she turned red. She felt like a rainbow, experiencing all the colors of the universe. Blue-cold with fear one second, red-hot with embarrassment the next. "I broke up with someone. It made him mad."

"The gentleman's name?"

"Kick Mitchell."

"Kick?"

"I mean, Robert. He goes by Kick."

Mr. Brehman shook his head and rubbed his chin. "No, that is not the gentleman."

He sat behind his desk and swiveled until she could only see the top of his balding head over the back of the chair. "You are dismissed. I will discuss it with you later."

"Sir? It's Friday."

"Yes, you will have to wait until Monday."

Maddy sat as if frozen.

"You are excused."

Maddy left, feeling the secretary's eyes boring into her back.

14

Maddy stepped inside The Cup & Chaucer. The gray, over-cast day made the light dim, and it felt evil and foreboding rather than cozy. She hoped the dim lighting would keep everyone from noticing her puffy eyes.

"You're early," Brad said.

Maddy nodded without expression and took off her cape.

"We can't pay for early hours," he reminded her. His voice sounded firm, but his expression was gentle and concerned.

"I'm a customer," she said quietly.

Brad's imposing lumberjack form bent over the bar. "One in dire need of a listening ear."

Maddy shook her head, the tears starting to fall again.

"Ahh," Brad nodded knowingly. "A listening ear away from other listening ears."

He came from behind the bar and took her by the elbow. "This way."

"But you can't leave...."

Brad looked around the corner into the main part of the cof-fee house. "Sam. Watch stuff for me, would ya? Tell the folks to wait a minute. I'm on a short break."

Brad gently directed Maddy all the way out the back door. The rain beat a solid, steady rhythm upon the canvas overhang. Their breath hung in clouds in front of their faces.

Brad cut right to the chase. "Look, Maddy. I care for you a bunch. Unfortunately, I can't stay out here for too long. So spit it out. You can't keep stuff like this to yourself." Brad stood with his arms crossed, his feet spread apart. He looked like a symbol of strength.

The story came out in torrents. And it didn't take long.

Brad pressed his lips together and nodded slowly. "Remember what I said a week ago?"

"Yes." Maddy hung her head.

"Am I to believe you really didn't participate?" His tone demanded the truth.

"How long was I gone?" Maddy said, chin up, eyes defiant. "How many other times have you smelled weed on me? Did I come in and start munching?"

Brad smiled.

"What did I say when I came in last night?"

Brad's grin grew to fill his face. "Yep. You're the girl I thought you were."

"You believe me?" Maddy felt no one would trust her story.

"Last week, I knew you hadn't smoked anything. But I wanted to make sure you were aware what others would think. And yes, you came in glowing last night. Wearing that pin like it was made of diamonds. I think I know that you don't lie. Let's go in. Your teeth are chattering."

As they walked through the hallway, Maddy said, "I'm so scared. What can I do?"

"I don't have the answer to everything, Maddy. I wish I did." Brad stopped before they reached the bar. "I promise I will think about it. If I come up with anything wonderful, I'll let you know."

Maddy touched his arm. "It means a lot that you believe me."

Maddy stumbled through the weekend. She dreaded Gram's phone call, so conveniently wasn't in her room at eleven. She hoped Mr. Brehman would not worry her grandmother until he had the whole situation straightened out. At The Cup & Chaucer, Brad didn't try to cheer Maddy up. He let her work hard, giving her extra tasks to keep her busy.

She didn't see much of Sarah. Maddy avoided being in the room except to sleep—taking long walks in the rain, exploring the campus and surrounding neighborhoods.

Church gave her a place to pray without being disturbed. Maddy began to feel peace mingled with her incredible nervousness. At the moment it was comfort that God knew the truth.

On Monday, she faced her finals with ambivalence. Part of her didn't even want to try. The other part wanted to do her best so that if she had to leave the school, she could at least leave with a good grade point average. Before the tests, she asked God to help her remember the stuff she knew.

She skipped lunch and went straight to the Dean's office after her second final. The secretary wore the same sour expression on her face, as if Maddy totally disgusted her, or her job did.

Maddy paused at the office door, her knees weak and

spongy. Dean Brehman chatted on the phone. He waved Maddy in, motioning her to sit. Maddy perched on the edge of her chair, covering her bare belly with her hand. Wanting to be polite and not eavesdrop, she started looking around the room. Then, afraid that also would be an invasion of privacy, she stared at her clasped hands. She figured she should be praying, but not a single word came to her. "Oh, God," she would start. And stop. Then she'd try again. The only thing that helped her to do was to not listen to Mr. Brehman.

Finally, silence made her look up. Mr. Brehman had hung up the phone and was leaning forward in his chair, hands folded on the desk, looking intently at her.

Maddy looked at him through saucer eyes.

"An unusual thing happened this morning."

Maddy nodded slowly, an encouragement for him to keep talking. Her mind raced. *Tell me I'm expelled. Just tell me. Don't give me stories that don't relate to anything.* But she kept silent. She squeezed her hands together in a death grip.

"I received a visit from several people on your behalf." Mr. Brehman looked at Maddy expectantly, as if she knew who had been there.

Maddy raised her brows. Her heart picked up speed.

At that moment, the intercom buzzed. "A gentleman is here to see you," Ms. Sour Face stated.

"I'm busy with Ms. MacDonald," Mr. Brehman replied.

"This is in regard to her situation," the secretary told him.

"Who is it?"

"Mr. Jason Stone."

Mr. Brehman nodded, then looked at Maddy. "Send him in."

Maddy felt a flood of relief. *Jason's here to help.* Then, it dawned on her. What did Jason know? She hadn't told anyone but Brad. She was too humiliated. Too embarrassed. She turned to watch Jason's entrance.

"Thank you, Mary," Jason said over his shoulder as he entered the room.

Figures he'd know that beetle-eyed secretary, Maddy thought.

Jason wore slacks. She'd never seen him wear slacks. She didn't think he owned any. He also wore a long raincoat over a short-sleeved dress shirt. He ignored Maddy, walking straight to Mr. Brehman. He held out his hand and a firm handshake was exchanged. Maddy felt stupid. She'd never thought to shake Mr. Brehman's hand.

"Sit," Mr. Brehman said, indicating the blue leather wing chair next to Maddy's.

Jason sat. "Sir, I was sorry to hear that you were not going to take action in this particular situation."

Mr. Brehman gave Jason a hard look. "And why do you doubt my decision?"

"As I told you, sir. I saw the transaction with my own eyes...."

Maddy gasped. "You? It was you who did this to me?"

"You did it to yourself," Jason said, spitting out his words. "I knew you were trouble from the first moment I laid eyes on you. I knew you were not who you said you were. "

Maddy shook her head slowly. "Jason, will you *ever* let up? Or let yourself see the truth?" She turned to Mr. Brehman, tears streaming down her face. "Even though Jason hasn't really liked me from the start, I never would have thought he'd make this kind of assumption. But all that really doesn't matter, does it? It's my word against his, and I don't expect you would believe me over someone like Jason." She stood and began walking toward the door.

"Ms. MacDonald," Mr. Brehman said curtly. "I have not excused you."

Maddy returned to her chair. Next to her, Jason sat with his right ankle casually resting on his left knee.

"Mr. Stone, your arrival interrupted what I had to say to Ms. MacDonald. And I let you come in, knowing I would tell you the same thing. I would like both of you to be quiet and listen."

Maddy folded her hands in her lap. Jason's right foot came down on the floor and he put his hands on his knees.

"I had unusual visitors this morning. First some people who dressed in, uh, a rather unkempt manner."

Maddy held her breath.

"These stated they have known Maddy for only a little over a month. Yet they have observed a certain quality of honesty, openness, and generosity in her. They heard Maddy discussing her situation with her boss and wished to come in and tell me what they knew."

Mr. Brehman stood and began his pacing, arms behind his back. "At first, I was quite cautious. I wondered if Ms. Mac-Donald had asked them to come speak to me. Their story interested me, as it had details even Ms. MacDonald had neglected to tell me."

Mr. Brehman looked at Jason. "It seems Ms. MacDonald has been giving coffee and leftover tidbits of food to these homeless people since she began working at The Cup & Chaucer. On this particular night, there was an abundant amount of food Ms. MacDonald had been invited to give to the kids in her dorm. Yet she chose to give some homeless people a feast. And the generous tip given her by the owner of the store ended up in the hands of the homeless person Ms. MacDonald trusted the most—a Mr. Duckworth."

Maddy stared at her hands in her lap. She felt embarrassed that her simple love of helping people had become public knowledge.

"That evening, a Mrs. Jimenez had planned to give Ms. MacDonald something she had made for her as a token of gratitude. It was this exchange you happened upon, Mr. Stone."

Jason sucked in an audible breath. "And you believe these homeless people? You think they'd tell you the truth? They can't even take care of themselves. Hey. I've smelled marijuana on Maddy before. She can't deny that." Now Jason was trying to defend his own integrity.

Mr. Brehman looked at Maddy. "Young lady?"

"Yes, sir. I was dating a guy who was smoking, and a couple of times encouraged me to join him. It would be a lie to say I wasn't tempted. But I didn't know temptation was wrong. I thought actually giving in was the wrong." She looked at Jason, who stared straight ahead.

"Mr. Stone," the Dean said, "I spoke with a Mr. Plimco, owner of The Cup & Chaucer. It is from him I discovered the fact that the bills Ms. MacDonald gave Mr. Duckworth were, in fact, a tip. He also seemed pleasantly surprised that the leftover food from his party went to needy people rather than to increase someone's popularity. "But it was Mr. Borden who brought me the final proof," he said.

"Brad?" Maddy said in a surprised exhale.

"He is the manager of The Cup & Chaucer, Mr. Brehman," explained to Jason. "He told me how delighted Ms. MacDonald was with the gift from Mrs. Jimenez. He felt if she had just purchased drugs, she would have been quiet and secretive. He had no idea Ms. MacDonald had turned her tip over to Mr. Duckworth. He only smiled, and said, "That's my Maddy.""

"Everywhere I go, every person I ask has only positive things to say about Ms. MacDonald. The only proof you have, Mr. Stone, is visual, in the dark, down an alley. We have proof from eyewitnesses, and character witnesses, and the evidence of these crocheted ice skates." Maddy touched her shoulder where they were pinned. "Those skates were described in detail by Mrs. Jimenez. If she hadn't given them to Ms. MacDonald, she could not have related their unique characteristics."

Jason's head had dropped. He turned and looked at Maddy. "I'm sorry." His voice lacked complete sincerity. "I'll try to believe your story."

"I really hope you can," Maddy said softly. " I'm sorry I didn't listen to you about Kick. You were totally right and I broke up with him that day. I appreciate the fact that you cared enough to tell me I was headed in the wrong direction."

Mr. Brehman sat behind his desk. He leaned forward, smiling at Maddy. "Ms. MacDonald, I am proud that you are a part of our university. I'm sorry you had to endure a weekend of such stress. I hope it didn't harm your finals."

Maddy could swear she saw a tear forming in Jason's eye.

"Ms. MacDonald, you may be excused. Not one notation of

this will be on your record." The dean gave a nod to Maddy and she stood. As she closed the door behind her, she heard Mr. Brehman's deep voice. "Mr. Stone. You need a good lesson in…."

In the hallway, all the tension she held inside released in tears, laughter, and a prayer of thanks.

15

"What did you do to your hair?" Maddy shrieked when she walked into her room.

"You like it?" Sarah asked, turning her head from side to side.

"It's adorable. It's you. It's not you." Maddy walked all the way around her. She lifted several strands to check it out.

Sarah stuck her tongue out. "What do you mean it's not me?"

"It's not the Sarah from California."

Sarah grinned. "No, it's not. That's why I did it."

"Let me see." Maddy inspected the style, which shaped Sarah's hair on the sides and cut it to her ears. The stylist had shaved the back to the nape of her neck. The top was layered, giving her hair a bouncy and full look. "You look great. I like the burgundy. Permanent or wash-out color?" She plopped into her chair and piled her books on the desk.

"Thanks! It's temporary. I wanted to get it done before Thursday night. Are you coming?" Sarah settled on her bed, her back against the wall.

"What's Thursday night?" Maddy looked up from her books.

Sarah sighed heavily. "I knew you weren't listening! I've been telling you about it all week." She dropped onto the bed.

"Sorry," Maddy said, still looking at her books. "I've been kind of preoccupied with stuff."

"Yeah. So I've noticed. Like what?" Sarah's voice was edged with the hurt of being left out.

"Like breaking up with Kick and other stuff." Maddy looked at her books, jotting fake notes with her pencil. She didn't want to go into it all. The fewer people who knew, the better.

"What other stuff?" Sarah pushed. "You were in your own little world all weekend."

Maddy looked up. "Just stuff."

Sarah's face began to show anger. "Tell me," she demanded.

"Some of my life is private." Maddy felt badly. She knew Sarah just wanted to be a friend to her.

"Nice to know you include your roommate in all your problems." Sarah got up off the bed and went to the common room, slamming the door behind her.

Maddy tapped her pencil on the table, thinking. How could she make Sarah understand? She dropped the pencil on the desk and went to the door. Sarah was slumped on the sofa. "Sarah? I'm sorry. I can't include you in everything."

"Then I can't include you in the Delta Gamma Chi Christmas party Thursday night," Sarah said, crossing her arms over her stomach. She stared at the wall so all Maddy got was her profile.

Maddy leaned on the doorjamb. "Sarah, you can be mad if you want. But I am getting awfully tired of people getting mad because I'm not who they want me to be. I'm really sorry I let you down. I didn't want to. Sometimes there aren't a whole lot of options."

"I just felt left out," Sarah said, her voice calm. "I like being your friend."

Maddy moved to kneel in front of Sarah. "If it makes you feel any better, the only person I talked to was my boss because he was part of it. Okay?"

Sarah turned her head toward Maddy. "Okay."

Maddy could tell it wasn't completely okay. But right now she'd take what she could get.

That night the words of the Psalms seemed especially close. Like she could hold them. Like they were alive. She went to sleep—after crying out the rest of the tension—with a smile on her face.

Maddy awoke before her alarm went off, to the sound of rain pelting her window. A fierce wind drove the drops straight at the panes. It looked like someone pointed a hose at her window, letting it blast full force. Then the wind would slacken off, and the rain would fall in a normal direction again.

Maddy put on her cape and braved the wind, chatting with friends who shared their umbrellas with her on their way to class.

After lunch and her U.S. History final, she teamed up with a friend headed in the direction of the library. "Can I bum some cover off you?" she asked.

The girl smiled. "Sure. Just cross your fingers the wind

doesn't break this thing. It hasn't been very trustworthy."

They parted at the library, just as a gust of wind popped the umbrella inside out. "Sorry!" Maddy called.

The girl waved and ran to cover.

The lions on the front door had darkened under the slanted rain. Moisture brought out the details of the wood. *What truly hides inside is brought to the surface in a storm,* Maddy remembered hearing somewhere. She wasn't sure what that came from, but she liked it.

She checked in with Alma at the circulation desk. "Jason wants to talk with you," Alma said. "He seems quite upset about something. I've given permission for you to take all the time you need—as long as you make it up by staying longer at the end of the day."

Maddy nodded.

"He's in the binding room."

Maddy took a deep breath. She walked down the hall, turned the corner, then paused in front of the closed door and offered up a prayer without words.

"Come in," Jason said, answering her timid knock.

Maddy cracked the door. "Is it safe? Are there flying objects?"

"I should ask you that," Jason said. He was seated on a stool, saw in hand. "Come on in."

"Put the saw down, and maybe I will."

A little smile tugged the corners of his mouth. He laid down the saw and jumped off the stool. They both sat at the work table.

"I'm afraid to ask," Maddy said, truly nervous, but wanting the ordeal over quickly.

"Maddy, I...." Jason put his hands on the table and pressed

161

down. He looked at the table, not at her. "I was mad yesterday."

"Yeah," Maddy said.

"And I couldn't go to sleep last night. I wouldn't say this to too many people, because they'd think I was nuts—I think God was yelling at me. I tried to rationalize that what I saw in the alley was the truth. The more I thought about what Dean Brehman said, the more I realized I have been a world-class jerk."

Maddy blinked, afraid to move, to do anything.

"I made a decision about you once. And that decision has colored everything you have done since."

"What about Thanksgiving? I thought things changed then. I thought you saw me for who I really am."

Jason softly tapped his fingers slow, and one at a time, on the table. "I tried then. And I did see some stuff." He sighed. "I guess I did a dumb guy thing. It really hurt me that you didn't listen to me about Kick. I finally got up enough nerve to maybe care about you as a person, and you snubbed me."

"I'm sorry about that, Jason." She bit her bottom lip, then decided to go ahead with what she had to say. "You snubbed me every moment I saw you. Why are you surprised that you would be snubbed?"

Jason kicked the floor with his heel. He picked at an old glue glob stuck on the table. "Look, Maddy. I'm afraid to say this." He took a deep breath. "I think I could learn a lot from you. I would never have spent time with those homeless people. Gave them something to eat? Yeah. Prayed for them? Yeah. But to be honest, I would probably just see them as grungy losers. You saw them as people. I didn't. Just like I didn't see *you* as a person." He put his head on the table, and his shoulders began to shake.

Maddy couldn't believe her eyes. Guys didn't cry if they could help it—and very few ever did in front of her. Jason's tears didn't last long, which Maddy was glad for. She never did know what she were supposed to do when a guy cried.

He looked at her, his eyelashes darkened by tears. "I am really, really sorry. I've asked God to forgive me, and I think he told me I have to ask you."

Maddy got up and walked around the table. She leaned over and put her arm across Jason's shoulders. "Of course I forgive you, you jerk."

"Thanks," Jason said, his voice husky.

"So, now I can say hi to you when I see you and eat with you in the dining hall and all that?"

Jason looked relieved. "Yeah. I'd like that."

"Cool." Maddy smiled and left the small room. "Close the door?" she asked over her shoulder.

Jason nodded. Maddy could see a few leftover tears lurking about his eyes as she left him there.

Alma scurried out from her desk. "Maddy, is everything all right?"

Maddy smiled. "Yeah, Alma," she said. "Everything is just fine."

That night, two friends from Starbucks and from school— Trina and Jeannie—called Maddy and asked her to go Christmas shopping with them. "Thanks, guys," Maddy said. "But I'm not sure I'll be real great to shop with."

"Have you done your shopping yet?" Trina asked.

"I've been avoiding it."

"Why?"

Maddy sighed. "Christmas only reminds me of what I don't have."

"So come with us anyway. We'll have fun."

Maddy decided to go and attempt to find something for Sarah and her grandmother. There was no use looking for her family. She didn't know where they were. And besides, her parents hated anything that would weigh them down and make it difficult to move easily.

On Wednesday, the girls met Maddy after her work at the library was done.

They stopped and had a Johnny Rocket burger, then dipped into every store in the nearby mini mall. At one shop, Trina and Jeannie picked out a dress for Maddy they insisted she try on. Maddy felt funny trying on something that would actually cover her mid-section. But when she put it on, she knew she'd found something special. Made in India, it was of a sheer fabric, with a thin lining underneath. It had patterns like wildflowers scattered everywhere. On Maddy, it looked perfect—long and flowing, the panels spreading out when she moved.

"You look absolutely fab, Maddy!" Trina said, her high pitched voice even higher.

"Look at this," Jeannie said. She plopped a black felt hat with a flower on Maddy's head.

At that moment, Maddy felt comfortable. Just like she used to in her old clothes before Jason came along.

Jeannie stood back and observed. "It's a must-buy."

"I don't know," Maddy told her. "I love it. It's just that I don't know if I should. I'm on a real tight budget." She kept looking over her shoulder in the mirror. She turned slowly to look again at the front.

Jeannie and Trina smiled at each other. "Well. Not a *real* tight budget."

"Excuse me?" Maddy stopped moving back and forth in front of the mirror.

"We've been assigned by someone to buy you something you liked." They looked at each other again and smiled at their shared secret.

Maddy put her hands on her hips. "Who?"

"We can't tell," Trina said. She moved to another rack filled with short dresses. She took a black one and held it up to herself.

"Then forget it." Maddy took off the hat, unhappy with the way life had to be.

"Look, he can afford it, okay?" Jeannie said. She put the hat back on Maddy's head.

"He?" Maddy said. She suddenly felt funny in the dress.

Trina smiled broadly. "He never said she couldn't guess." She replaced the dress on the rack and chose one of forest green.

Jeannie pointed at her. "You have a point."

"Think, Maddy," Jeannie said. "Who would want you to have a Christmas bonus?"

Maddy cocked her head. "Brad?"

"Who's Brad?" Jeannie asked.

"Forget it. It couldn't be him." Maddy tried to think. For the life of her, she couldn't imagine who would buy her a dress.

"He's real proud of you," Trina hinted.

It clicked. "Mr. Plimco?" Maddy asked, astounded.

The girls nodded. Jeannie popped a beret onto her own head, checking out the look in the mirror.

"Why didn't he just give me a bonus like a normal boss?" Maddy asked. It still felt like her jaw was hanging on a loose hinge.

"He wouldn't tell us. He just said you did something real special and hoped we wouldn't be mad that you would get a bigger bonus," Trina said. "I'm dying to know what you did. I could use a new outfit."

"But, how? When?"

"Joe heard us talking at work about going shopping and said he wanted to send us on a secret mission."

"But you guys deserve something, too," Maddy told them.

"Look. Joe is fair. We trust him. He'll probably take us to dinner sometime and that'll be just as fun," Trina said. Jeannie nodded enthusiastically.

Maddy decided to wear the dress home, and packed up her leggings and shortie top in the shopping bag. She felt different walking down the mall. She felt good. Special. She also felt people looked at her in a new way. The guys walking by didn't seem to gobble her up. They showed her looks of appreciation instead.

She scoured the stores, searching for something to buy. Like every other year, she tried to ignore the effort to remind the world that Christmas was about families. Cozy families who got

166

together to share warmth and love and memories and traditions. Loving families who ate big meals cooked and served by the matriarchs of those families. Maddy hated feeling left out. She hated the reminders of all she didn't have.

At a video store, she asked the clerk about classic movies and bought one called *It's a Wonderful Life*. The clerk assured her it would be perfect for Gram's collection, and Trina and Jeannie agreed.

It took her awhile to decide what to get for Sarah, but when she found the gift, she knew it was perfect. It was so perfect, it lifted her spirits just a little to think that she was doing one thing right.

Thursday sped by, with Maddy getting tons of compliments on her casual dress and hat. Jason looked at her with a startled glance, then looked away quickly.

Back in the room, Sarah was trying to pack for her plane trip the next morning. She muttered and grumbled between streaks of excitement about the evening's party.

"I don't want to go home, Maddy. They're all idiots," Sarah said as she dug through her dresser drawers.

"Sarah!"

"It's true. They raised me to live like a nun. You wouldn't understand. You were brought up to be free and do what you want. I've had to dress a certain way, think a certain way, act a certain way. Like if I did anything different, lightning would come and strike me down. It's all a lie, and I'm not going to live like that anymore."

"What does this ranting and raving have to do with Christmas?" Maddy asked.

Sarah threw down a pile of underwear into her suitcase. "Everything! When I go home, my parents are going to freak about my new clothes. They're going to freak about my haircut. They are going to freak about absolutely everything."

Maddy smiled and curled up with her pillow. "I see. Family really is important."

"No. I'm angry at them. They've stifled me, Maddy. And I'm ticked off."

"I don't want to sound like an old fogy, but Sarah, you are really lucky to have family. It doesn't matter if they're relaxed about life or the ultimate straights."

"Maddy, you just don't know. You don't have to see the same stupid people every year and listen to the same old stories and watch everybody being so polite to each other when they barely speak the rest of the year."

Maddy closed her eyes, trying to imagine how wonderful that would be. "Do they all hug you when they get there?"

"Yes. And when they leave. And when they open a present."

Maddy's longing grew deeper. "Do you feel kind of tied to all that?" she asked, her eyes still closed.

"Tied up, strangled."

"You really don't know how lucky you are."

Sarah threw shoes into her suitcase as hard as she could. "Let's change the subject."

"I don't know if I'll really have a chance to see you before you go to your party tonight," Maddy said.

Sarah froze. "What? You aren't going?"

"No. I think I'll skip it." The last thing Maddy wanted to do was to go to a party and face her temptations head on.

"Just because Kick is going to be there?"

Maddy sat up. "That's part of it."

Sarah sat on Maddy's bed. "You've got to come. There're so many great guys who are going to be there."

"Thanks, but no thanks." Maddy reached under her pillow and made sure Sarah's package was still there. "Do you think you'll have time to have dinner with me tonight before you go to the party? I thought we'd have kind of a good-bye thing."

"Yeah. Help me choose what to wear, and then I'll be ready."

"What about your packing?"

"That can wait. Let's blow this place."

16

Sarah borrowed all of Maddy's bracelets for the occasion. She put on her own new black leggings with a forest green top that had all sorts of loopy threads all over it. It looked glamorous, and with her new haircut, Sarah was stunning.

They walked to Mama Giordino's. Restaurants like this made Maddy adore Seattle. Tucked into a small shop, it didn't look like much on the outside. On the inside, it was decorated in a way that made her feel she had been transported to Italy. Red and white checkered tablecloths were, of course, a requirement. Maps of Italy, beaded dresses, murals, and fat jugs covered with straw completed the picture. Maddy figured the best pasta in the world must be served right here.

Mama seated them in the front of the restaurant at the window. Maddy loved watching the people walk by as they ate. After ordering shrimp with linguine and alfredo sauce, Maddy reached into her bag and pulled out the small package she had hidden there. "Here." She put it on the table in front of Sarah. "Merry Christmas."

"I didn't bring yours! You should have told me."

"It's okay. Open it."

Sarah slipped the shredded, curly ribbon off the small box and opened it. "Oh!" she exclaimed taking out the earrings. One was a little stick man, the other a stick woman. They were pieced together at important joints so they jiggled almost like real people. Then Sarah's face fell.

"I know what you're thinking," Maddy said. "You don't have pierced ears. That's part of your gift. If you eat fast enough, we'll have time to get them pierced before the party. I found this place that has cool piercing studs. You can choose the ones you want."

"And I only got you a dumb old umbrella," Sarah said.

Maddy laughed. "There are plenty of people at the U who will be delighted to hear that."

After a sumptuous dinner, they practically ran all the way to the indoor mall where Sarah chose earrings with a tiny cubic zirconia surrounded by equally tiny pearls. "They're perfect for the party tonight."

The girls walked arm in arm to the Gamma Kappa Phi house. The party had already started. Music boomed in a steady beat out into the street. "Please come," Sarah encouraged. "I really want you here. I want to introduce you to everyone."

Maddy hesitated. She looked up at the house, a large, old brick mansion with two massive white pillars out front. Why didn't she want to go in? Why was her heart not in it anymore?

"You love parties, Maddy. I know you do. Come on."

At the top of the stone stairs someone opened the door as if he had been waiting for them. "Hey, Maddy! Sarah! Come on in. Sarah, Joel is looking for you. Down the hall. Back living room."

Maddy tried to mentally shift into party gear as she felt Sarah pull her along. But it was like the last party with Kick. She didn't feel comfortable. All her guilt from the past party swarmed over her. She felt suffocated. She wanted to run for her life. She kept telling herself she was here for Sarah. Doing a good thing for Sarah to help her open up and be able to tackle life on her own. It sounded like a lie. Helping Sarah become a party girl? Maddy didn't want Sarah to end up like the party kids. How could she justify her being here at all?

All parties are not bad.

She forced herself to look around. The partiers seemed to be hanging out, rather than doing the 'party animal' thing. She relaxed a little.

In the back living room, the kids weren't smoking, so the air was clear. A set of speakers was wired into that room also, so the music was just as loud. A short, stocky Korean kid came to Sarah, licking his lips as he saw her. "Well, you *did* come."

Sarah smiled shyly. All her exuberance about the party disappeared when she walked in.

Maddy nudged her.

"Hi, Joel," was all Sarah could manage.

"You've always been a bit on the quiet side, Sarah, but I'm not used to you being this shy. Come on. Open up. These are your friends." He grabbed a bottle from a nearby tub. "Here's your beer."

Sarah stared at the beer in her hand. "I…uh…don't drink," she managed to say, but Joel had already gone.

"You don't have to drink beer. I'm sure they have Coke somewhere." Maddy dug around in the metal tub and found a can of pop. She stuck it in Sarah's hand, deciding to help her through. "Okay. Now let's join the group."

Around them, several students debated about whether or not the people of America had voted in the right president. "They're talking about stuff you have an opinion on," Maddy urged Sarah. "You can do it."

Maddy walked up to the group. "Do you think Whitewater affected the outcome?"

She dove into the conversation, not really having a clue about a lot of the political ins and outs, but enjoying tossing out her own ideas anyway. After awhile, she moved over to Sarah, who hadn't moved. "Come on," Maddy said, "Let's go." She took Sarah's hand and started to leave the room.

Something seemed to snap in Sarah. "No! I'm staying." She yanked her hand away.

"You haven't said five words to anyone. If you feel uncomfortable here, that's okay. We can find other ways to be with people. This isn't your kind of thing."

Sarah moved a fraction of a foot toward the gap on the sofa.

"Please, let's go," Maddy gently encouraged. "You don't need this. It's stupid for you to torture yourself like this."

"No," Sarah said. "The closed off way I've been raised is stupid." She marched over to Joel and put her hand into the crook of his arm. "I want to have fun," she said loudly.

Joel smiled his approval. "You bet."

"Let's dance."

"Okay," Joel said, leading her from the room.

Maddy stayed with the conversation a little while longer until the students started talking foreign policy. This was out of her league for certain. She wandered around the house. All around her, students were having deep conversations or swapping crazy stories. Sarah danced. Everyone was having a ball.

Suddenly, Maddy felt very, very tired. She didn't belong here. Didn't really want to belong. She sidled up to Sarah. "I'm going. Please come."

"Are you kidding?" Sarah shouted over the music. "I'm having way too much fun. Send a stretcher for me in the morning."

Maddy looked around the room. It was probably the cleanest party she'd ever been to. She hadn't seen any drugs or hard liquor. She decided it wasn't much different from Sarah's church parties, except for the beer and dancing.

"Be careful, huh?" she said to Sarah.

"Are you kidding? Yeah!"

Maddy didn't like leaving Sarah. Something told her not to. But she didn't know what else to do. She decided if she really left, then maybe Sarah would follow.

Maddy went home, but she couldn't sleep. She was attacked by thoughts about Christmas and belonging and Sarah not acting like Sarah. Finally, she gave up on sleep and opened another autobiography she'd picked up at the library—*Not Without My Daughter*. She started to read, and the woman's story gripped her almost immediately.

She had no clue how long she had been reading when Sarah came in. Maddy looked up. Mascara streaked Sarah's pale face. She looked unkempt, but in a subtle way. Her sweater had shifted a tiny bit.

"Talk to me," Maddy said, putting the book down. "What happened?"

Sarah bit her trembling lower lip and shook her head.

"Oh, Sarah," Maddy said. She stood up and put her arms around her. "Come here."

With that, Sarah started bawling. Maddy led her to the bed and sat down next to her.

"I just wanted to have fun," Sarah said between her sobs.

Maddy's heart felt sick. "You were having fun when I left, weren't you?" *I knew I shouldn't have left her.*

Sarah nodded.

"Then what happened?" Maddy handed Sarah a Kleenex and waited for her to blow.

"I only drank one beer," Sarah said. "There's nothing terrible about that, is there?"

"I'm not sure," Maddy said. She repeatedly kicked herself. She should have encouraged Sarah to stick with the Coke. Should have prepared her better.

Tear's streamed down Sarah's cheeks. "And Joel kept telling me I looked so pretty and so sexy." The pain in Sarah's voice sounded like that of betrayal. Maddy felt a chill. "No one's ever told me that before."

"What did you do?" Maddy asked her, afraid to know the answer.

"I said, 'Thanks,' and smiled up at him." She paused, snuffling a little. "And then he kissed me."

"And that was…?"

Sarah smiled through her tears. "Wonderful."

"So then what happened?"

"We danced some more, and then other guys wanted to dance with me. And then they had two guys dancing with me. And I thought it was all okay still. I thought it was kind of funny—I'd never seen people dance like that—kind of like a sandwich. And then Joel grabbed me and kissed me hard, and then he…put his hand…" her tears poured out fresh. "He put his hand on me. I shoved it away, and he did it again. And then another guy took me and danced, and he put his hand on me, and I tried to tell them to stop it."

"Why didn't they?" Maddy asked in a whisper.

"They said I wanted it. They could tell because of the way I moved. And the way I danced. And the way I dressed."

Maddy didn't understand.

"Kick was there. He seemed high. He took me aside, while all the time the guys kept laughing and pointing at me. He told me that I was giving messages to the guys that I was easy. I couldn't believe it. Me? Easy? Not me, Maddy. I just wanted to have fun. I just wanted to get to know people. I told Kick that and he shook his head and said if I couldn't handle it I should run home to Mama and be a baby."

"So you left?"

Sarah nodded. "I'm so mixed up, Maddy. I don't get it." She snuffled and blew her nose again. She wadded up the sopping tissue and tossed it toward the waste basket. She missed. Sarah took another tissue and wrung it in her hands. "Why can't I have fun? Why do I have to ruin everything?"

Maddy shook her head, thoughts swarming inside. "Go wash up. Take a shower. Put on your flannel nightie. I'll have some hot cocoa ready when you get back."

Sarah grabbed her things and left the room.

Maddy went down the hall to the common room to put a mug of water into the small microwave. She tried to straighten out the thoughts that ran into each other, confusing her. Was Jason right? Did clothes really make a difference? She knew her clothes attracted guys. But did they think she was advertising for something she wasn't necessarily selling? Or was it that she had dressed like that for so long, it didn't give off the same messages? Sarah dressed in Maddy's clothes got far different reactions than Maddy did. Was it wrong for Sarah to wear clothes like that?

Maddy couldn't sort anything out that really made sense. Back in their room, she added instant cocoa to the hot water and stirred. In a drawer, she found a few small marshmallows left in the bottom of a plastic bag and dumped them all on top of the cocoa.

Sarah walked behind her to the living room, wrapped in her robe, her hair in a towel. She plopped onto the sofa and lifted her hands for the cocoa. "Why did they act like that? Are they animals?"

"Sometimes people are rude. Guys can get rowdy when they've had too much to drink." Maddy swallowed hard. "I think this is partly my fault, Sarah."

"How can you say that?"

"I forgot that some guys take advantage of naive girls." Maddy curled herself on the sofa. "The dance you thought was fun and innocent was actually a kind of a testing ground."

Sarah sipped the cocoa. "What do you mean?"

"Since you didn't object to the first sensuous dance, they probably figured you wouldn't object to anything else."

Sarah grew pale.

"I think you and I made a big mistake. I think we thought you were somebody else."

"Speak English," Sarah said, her voice no more than a whisper.

"Your clothes. Your hair. Going to a party like this. Did we think we could fool everyone into thinking you are someone you aren't? Or are you trying to force *yourself* into being someone you really aren't?"

"You wear clothes like this," Sarah said, irritation rising in her voice.

"These clothes are part of my personality," Maddy said quietly. "I've worn them for years. They say I'm different."

"And you think you're the only person who can dress that way?"

Maddy tucked her feet underneath her and dragged the afghan off the back of the sofa to cover her legs. "Of course not."

"Then why can't I dress like you?" Sarah's eyes held fire in them.

"You can dress however you want," Maddy said kindly. "It's just that I wonder if you are trying to make yourself into someone you're not. We both made a mistake in thinking it doesn't matter how you dress. It *does* matter. What you wear tells others who you are. And I'm beginning to wonder—just tonight—whether or not I should be making some changes in how *I* dress."

"I want people to like me the way they like you. I want to be as comfortable with people as you are," Sarah said, setting down her empty mug.

"Those things don't come with the clothes," Maddy said softly. "Those things come with being comfortable with who you are." Maddy pushed her hair back from her face. "Look. Maybe instead of trying to teach you to be someone you aren't we should teach you how to make the best of the characteristics God has given you."

"So I can't wear my new clothes any more?"

"Wear whatever you want. But instead of wearing what your mother wants you to wear, or what someone you admire wears, why not try on tons of stuff until you figure out what *you* like to wear?"

Sarah nodded. "Will you help me?"

Maddy tipped back her head and laughed. "I doubt I'll be much help. I can go with and tell you if you look pasty or like a dunce. But other than that, you'll have to figure it out on your own."

"When we get back. I'll save all my Christmas money."

Maddy nodded. "First day before classes."

Sarah put her feet on the coffee table. She put her hand to the towel and unwrapped her hair. "My family really isn't so bad, Maddy. I'm trying to figure out who I am and I guess that's just making me a little crazy." Sarah stood. "I'll find where I fit and who I am. I'll just try not to push so hard."

"Good!" Maddy said. She dramatically put the back of her hand to her brow. "I cannot take much more of this pendulum's sweep."

"Oh, shush!" Sarah said. "Like you never go to extremes."

"*Moi?* Never!"

Both girls laughed.

Maddy stood. They hugged briefly. Together they went into their room. Sarah finished packing while Maddy read.

Maddy lost track of time until she heard a faint rumble coming from Sarah. She looked up. Sarah was asleep, an open book next to her, the reading light burning up watts.

Maddy smiled and turned off the light.

17

Maddy carried her things in three bags down the stairs to where her grandmother waited for her in her car. Maddy felt more awkward than ever. Her heart picked up speed. Who was this woman, really?

Gram stood outside the car, waiting, a black umbrella keeping her from getting soaked. Maddy looked at her, wondering what was the proper form of action to take. Hug? Be aloof? Gram's face mirrored Maddy's questions.

"Hi, Gram. Thanks for coming to get me," Maddy said, trying to be warm and friendly.

"Let's put the bags in the back seat. Then the bike will fit in the trunk," Gram said matter-of-factly.

Maddy nodded and did as she was told. She shut the trunk on the bike, and slipped into the front seat of the car. "I'm dripping on your seat, Gram."

"It's been dripped on plenty of times before." Gram looked over her shoulder as she pulled from the parking space. Nothing more was said until they drove by The Cup & Chaucer.

"Is that where you work?" Gram asked.

"Yes." Maddy watched it go, wishing she felt the same comfort with her Gram as she did with The Cup.

"Do you like it?" Gram was trying hard to make conversation. Was she just being polite? Or was she really interested?

"I like it a lot." Maddy bit the inside of her cheek. How could she reach out? What if Gram was only tolerating her?

She looked at Gram. She had her hands placed perfectly in the 10 and 2 positions on the steering wheel. Each move she made was precise. The click of the turn signal. The click of the windshield wipers. Her wheel turning to go around the corners. Was she being quiet because she had nothing to say to her granddaughter? Or was she the quiet type anyway, who would enjoy someone's company with or without talk? How could Maddy be related to this stranger?

The virtual silence carried through the afternoon and dinner. The only time Maddy really got any kind of reaction from her grandmother was in the early afternoon. Maddy had gone to the kitchen for some coffee. All she could see of Gram was her ample posterior sticking out from behind the refrigerator door. "Maddy?" Gram had said, her hands still moving things around. "Would you like to cook dinner this evening?"

Maddy laughed. Gram removed herself from the refrigerator. "Is that a yes?"

"I don't know how to cook. Thanksgiving was a stretch for me. I couldn't have done my part without your help. But if you want frozen dinners or macaroni and cheese, I'll be delighted to whip some up for you."

Gram put her hands on her hips. "You don't know how to cook? Why Maddy MacDonald, that's a disgrace."

Maddy felt chastised. "I'm sorry. I never really had the chance."

"Well that's going to change!" Gram went back to her rummaging and didn't say another word. Maddy fixed her coffee and returned to her room.

The next morning after the breakfast dishes had been done, Maddy wiped her sweaty palms on the apron Gram had draped and tied around her neck. "I've never really made anything before."

"You've said that plenty of times. I think I understand it now," Gram said. "It's high time you learned."

"What's the point, anyway?" Maddy said, pouting. She didn't want anyone to see how clumsy she could be.

"The point is you'll need to survive on your own someday." Something zinged through Maddy. Was this her grandmother caring about her?

"I'll eat out," Maddy said dryly.

"And weigh two thousand pounds before you're forty, and be broke."

Maddy sighed heavily. "Make this as painless as possible, please."

Gram shook her head. "You'd think I was taking the kid to a dentist." She slapped her hands together. "Where's the recipe?"

"Here." Maddy held it up.

"It's an old family recipe. The things I teach you are secret, and you are never to tell another soul."

Maddy nodded. *Gram is trusting me with a family secret? This is absolutely incredible!* Her heart warmed. *This is too special. I'm going to listen and try to do at least an okay job. I hope she'll still speak to me after I've butchered the secret family recipe.*

"Read the recipe carefully." Gram spoke as a careful teacher. "When you first start cooking, it's a good idea to line up all the ingredients in a row on the counter. That way you won't forget anything."

Maddy trembled as she read the first ingredient. "Cream cheese."

Gram nodded. "How much?"

"16 oz."

"That means sixteen ounces." She opened the refrigerator door and pointed to two silver boxes. "Look here. On the label. Eight ounces each."

Maddy felt like a little kid doing her first craft in kindergarten. All thumbs. Her grandmother walked her through each step, patient and even-toned. Not like Maddy's mother. Her mother shrieked and got frustrated easily, so Maddy had stopped asking her to help her learn anything. Maddy was seventeen before she realized her mother usually didn't know how to do it either, and was shrieking at herself as much as she was shrieking at her daughters.

But Gram touched Maddy gently on the elbow. She brushed Maddy's hair away from her cheek. She encouraged Maddy when she got it right. They laughed at Maddy's jokes when she got it wrong. Maddy almost felt like she was being drawn into Gram's inner circle. This, perhaps, was Gram's language of love.

A little over an hour later, Maddy withdrew a cheesecake masterpiece from the oven. "I did this?" she asked, incredulous.

Gram nodded, her face beaming. "And wait until you taste it."

Maddy picked up a knife.

"NO!" Gram said. "A cheesecake is no good unless you refrigerate it overnight."

Maddy sighed and childishly stomped her foot. "I'm going to have to wait until tomorrow to eat the blasted thing?"

Gram nodded.

"You should have told me," Maddy said. She pouted at the dessert.

"Some things have to wait, Maddy," Gram told her. "Waiting makes them better."

The whole cooking thing opened two doors inside Maddy. One reminded her of all that she didn't have with a family. The other door opened to hope that she would find some kind of family someday. In response to her thoughts, Maddy blurted out, "You could wait a lifetime for a family and never get one."

"You have a family," Gram said, her hand reaching out, then falling to her side.

Maddy looked at her grandmother as she untied the apron strings. "Not really."

"You do," Gram insisted.

"I have a family in name. Sure. I have a mother and a father and two sisters. Are we a family? Are we connected? Do I have anything to show for my life? A home? A house? There's nowhere Gram. Nothing that I can point to that says I belong. Or I connect. Or I've been there."

Gram stiffened. "I don't like this kind of talk. I think we should change the subject."

"Fine. Ignore the truth if you want. I can't. This hole right here," Maddy tapped her chest, "reminds me of it all the time."

"I said enough."

Maddy flung the apron down onto the counter. She spun around and marched to her room. She flung herself on the bed. An ache made her want to cry. Anger made her want to storm her parents' apartment—wherever that was—and tell them off.

She rolled over and looked at the canopy overhead. A filmy, gauzy fabric spanned the gap between the bedposts. It reminded her of her family—there, but not terribly functional.

Would she hear from them on Christmas? In two days, she would know. Gram had asked her to attend the Christmas Eve candlelight service at her church the next night. Maddy agreed to go. Now she wondered if she could stand seeing all those loving families.

She hated Christmas more than anything. Her joy of life slipped away every year at this time. She hated knowing that families all around her were bustling about, making Christmas plans, wrapping Christmas gifts. Maddy had wrapped her one present for Gram at school, bumming off someone else's roll of Christmas wrap. She'd bought her sisters each a pair of funky Space Needle earrings, which she would save until she saw them again. Her parents had told her before that Seattle was the one city they would never live in. They would never visit.

She had to stop thinking like this. She had to stop making herself miserable. Maddy opened the nightstand drawer and took out her book. *Love is Eternal*. She never thought much about Abe Lincoln. This book opened his world like she'd never expected, and she escaped to another time when it wasn't Christmas.

On Christmas Eve, Maddy told Gram to open her present early —right after dinner. Gram was so excited about her gift, the movie, that they decided to pass the evening watching Jimmy Stewart before their church service.

Maddy served them each a large slice of cheesecake on a pretty china plate. She brewed some tea for Gram and a cup of coffee for herself while Gram got the TV and VCR ready.

Gram refused to put the movie on until Maddy had tried her cheesecake.

"It's no big deal, Gram."

"Sure it is. It's your first attempt. It's our secret family recipe. It's a great big deal and don't you forget it. Now take your bite." Gram watched Maddy with great anticipation. Maddy almost couldn't put the bite in her mouth with Gram staring at her like that.

"Stop it!" Maddy said through her giggles. "You're making me laugh and I can't eat if you're making me laugh."

Gram pursed her lips and jutted her chin toward Maddy. "Eat up, young lady. Eat up."

Maddy laughed even harder. She finally managed to slip the bite into her mouth. Automatically her eyes closed. "Ummm," she moaned. "This is so good."

She opened her eyes. Gram nodded like a toy puppy with its head on a spring, bobbing up and down in the back seat window of an old Chevy. "Isn't it great?"

"It's incredible!" Maddy said rudely, her mouth full of another bite of cheesecake. She leaned over and popped a slick kiss onto her grandmother's cheek. "Thank you, Gram." Maddy thought her heart would melt with gratitude. She couldn't believe she had made it. She dropped her fork on the plate. "Are you fooling me?"

Gram looked startled. "Whatever are you talking about?"

"Did you throw away my cheesecake and make it yourself so I'd feel good?"

Gram shook her head slowly. She put her soft hand on Maddy's knee. "Maddy dear. You have a lot of fine qualities. You did this all yourself. And you did good." Maddy felt warmth spreading through her.

Gram started the movie and Maddy ate her cheesecake. It was far too rich for her to eat the whole huge slice, so she set it down when she'd eaten half of it. Gram tugged Maddy's arm a little bit and Maddy moved closer. By the time the movie was over, Maddy had snuggled quite close, and sometimes rested her head on Gram's shoulder. Gram said nothing, and neither did Maddy. Yet a growing power seemed to draw them together.

The movie hit Maddy dead center. She thought about it while she dressed for church. Could it be? Could it be possible that her life could make a positive difference? She wondered. The sweet family scenes had made her feel uncomfortable. Yet, Jimmy Stewart's character wasn't all that thrilled about life, even though he had a good family.

She walked into church holding Gram's gloved hand. The old cathedral was awesome. Pillars of stone held up the arches. Stained glass windows told the story of the life of Jesus without a word. A manger scene dominated the front of the church. Silently, Maddy and Gram took their seats in the wooden pews.

She was glad they got there early enough to sit close to the front.

The service opened with a choir singing "Silent Night" a cappella. Maddy couldn't describe what she felt. Glory to God. A soaring in her spirit. A peace. A hope. As the story of Christmas unfolded in the scene before her, the nasty thoughts and feelings about Christmas took on a new light. She'd been looking at Christmas in the wrong way. Yes, this particular holiday made what she was missing in her life very clear. But this holiday also made it very clear what she *had*, too. This God she met had done the most incredible thing. Not only did his Son die for Maddy...but he also left what could only be a glorious heaven to come to earth to *live*.

Mary, Joseph, God-child. This was a family she could belong to. God adopted her. She wasn't without family.

Maddy knew all this before. But it had never really penetrated to her soul until now.

She lifted her face toward heaven. *Can we try again, God? I'll try to really listen to you as my Father. Thanks for showing me that the feeling I have for family is not crazy. Everything you've done revolves around family.*

Maddy was afraid to continue with what she wanted to say. Then she figured God knew what she hesitated about. She might as well tell him.

Since you've shown me I am a part of a family....I'm really glad and I don't want to offend you, but I still hope that you can somehow give me something I can touch and feel and belong to. Something or someone that is an earthly family.

Maddy lowered her eyes and stared at the baby in the

manger. She listened to the sounds of the live animals. *I'll never hate Christmas again*, she decided. She knew it wouldn't wash away the pain of what she didn't have. But now, Christmas became wide and full and marvelous. God had sent his Son.

Gram seemed to know something special had happened. She said nothing to Maddy all the way home.

Maddy slipped into bed feeling warm and loved.

18

Maddy didn't want to get out of bed. The down comforter kept her warm and cozy with just the right amount of weight on top of her. The only thing missing was a loving mom to hold her.

Gram rapped on the door softly. "Maddy? Are you awake, dear?"

"Yes, Gram."

"You stay snuggled for awhile. I'll get breakfast."

"Gram? Can you come in a minute?" Maddy quivered at what she was about to risk.

Gram opened the door and stepped inside.

"Can I have a hug?" Maddy asked shyly. She felt stupid, but she wanted one so desperately.

Gram moved across the room. She sat on the bed and Maddy sat up. Gram smelled of soap and flowers. Maddy wanted to be a little girl and hang on for a long time. But she was nineteen and had to let go. "Merry Christmas, Gram."

"Merry Christmas, Maddy."

"Do you want some help downstairs?" Maddy offered.

Gram held Maddy's hand between her own. Her hands were warm and dry, comforting. "I'd rather do it myself. I'll put on some Christmas carols right away. When I'm ready for you, I'll play 'Joyful, Joyful.'"

Maddy watched her grandmother leave. Even in her plush robe, she looked the elegant lady.

Taking her Bible, Maddy opened it to the index. She wanted to find where Luke was so she could read the same scripture the minister had read the night before. She found it.

Christmas carols performed by some orchestra wafted up the stairs, the sound mingling with the smells of eggs, sausage, cinnamon, and coffee. The aroma alone was enough to make Maddy race downstairs. Soon, she couldn't wait any more. She put a sweatshirt and sweatpants over her T-shirt and boxers, ran her fingers through her hair, and tiptoed down the stairs.

She poked her head in the kitchen, but Gram wasn't there. She went to the living room. Gram sat in a wing back chair, her back to Maddy. She had turned the tree lights on. Underneath were a very few wrapped packages. Maddy moved around the chair. Gram sat there, a photo album open on her lap. She held a hankie in one hand, but didn't use it for the tears dripping down her face.

"Gram?" Maddy asked quietly, kneeling beside the chair.

"Oh! You startled me." Gram snapped the photo album shut. She turned her face and dabbed her tears. "I guess I forgot about breakfast." She stood abruptly.

"Gram," Maddy said, staying beside the chair. "What's wrong?"

"Nothing."

Maddy followed her to the kitchen. Gram had set the dining room table with all the best china. Holly and berries mixed with angel hair lay between golden candlesticks formed like angels. White candles burned brightly. "Gram, it's beautiful. But you didn't have to go to all this trouble."

"I most certainly did," she said smartly. "It's Christmas. And I have been blessed with my granddaughter's presence."

Maddy smiled. "Can I help you bring in breakfast?"

"No you may not. I serve my special guests."

Gram brought out some kind of egg dish that stood tall and fluffy. Three pieces of browned sausage were laying next to each of the round, ceramic dishes the eggs were in. Next she put down a side plate that held a cinnamon roll topped with dark, runny cinnamon sauce. Maddy's coffee steamed in a mug.

After prayer, Maddy began her feast. Her grandmother's tears still bugged her. A great breakfast was not the place to bring up the subject, so she ate in silence.

As soon as she finished breakfast, Gram put an envelope on the table in front of her. "This came yesterday. I saved it so you would have something to open this morning."

Maddy stared at the envelope. Her mother's handwriting sprawled across the front. Tears blurred her vision just for a moment. She opened it quickly. A piece of white paper closed around money. "Well, Maddy," the letter said, "it's Christmas and we'll be missing you. We're in Grand Island, Nebraska, but won't be here long. Business is slow. So I didn't bother to enclose our address. Buy yourself something from us. Love, Mom."

Maddy dropped the letter on the table. No word about her

sisters. Nothing from her father. Just three ten dollar bills. She sat there and stared at them. The ache in her heart grew a little deeper and a little wider.

Gram's hand rested on Maddy's shoulder. "Not great, huh?"

Maddy shook her head.

"Some people are not capable of showing love. They are so caught up in their own desperate need, they have nothing left to give someone else."

Maddy nodded, knowing it was true, but wishing that for parents, it wasn't.

She stuffed the letter and money into the pocket of her robe and helped Gram wash dishes. Afterward, Gram untied her apron and said, "I want you to open your gifts now. Let's go to the living room."

Maddy followed Gram and sat on the sofa with her legs tucked underneath her. Gram sat in her wing back chair. For a few moments, they both sat, looking at the fire in the great fireplace. Antique Christmas knickknacks adorned the mantle, nestled in angel hair. A chain of solid gold stars draped from one side of the mantle to the other.

Ignoring her presents, Maddy ventured, "Gram, why can't we be close?"

Gram looked down at her hands and began to squeeze them together. Maddy saw her glance toward the photo album that still lay on the coffee table between them.

Maddy forced herself to ask her deepest question. "Am I so awful that you can't like me?"

"Oh, no!" Gram protested. "You are a delightful, wonderful young lady. You remind me so much of myself when I was young. So full of life, so willing to fly to the side of a friend or try new things. Nothing can hold you down."

"Except the rules of PCU's Admin Committee," Maddy said dryly.

Gram laughed, light and airy. "They are trouble, aren't they?"

"You mean you didn't tell them to put those rules on me?"

"Heavens, no. I thought they were ridiculous. I knew that if you had enough guts to call your excommunicated grandmother out of the blue to ask to come live with her, you had the moxy it would take to get yourself through a university like PCU."

Maddy nodded. "It wasn't easy to find you. I wasn't stupid. I knew I had grandparents somewhere. But I had no idea really who you were or anything."

"So how did you find me?"

Maddy screwed up her lips and stared down at her grandmother's slippered feet. "I was bad, Gram. I snooped in some old boxes at the back of Dad's closet. He always had this crazy box that he moved everywhere, but never unpacked. I knew he didn't unpack it because it was the same old box, year after year."

"Shame on you," Gram said without conviction. Then curiosity got the best of her. "What was in the box?"

"Not much. Mostly old drawings he must have saved since he was a kid. But there was one newspaper clipping about Grandfather being a part of the board of directors for PCU, and Grandfather's obituary." Maddy thought a moment. "How did he get those anyway?"

Gram stared into the distance. "The board of directors article would have been from when your father was still living at home. I don't know about the obituary. I had tried to contact him at that time, but failed."

"Anyway," Maddy continued her story, "I called Information, got PCU's phone number, and found you through them. It wasn't easy, though. They don't like to give out information about anything but their school."

"Why me, Maddy?"

Maddy put her hand on her grandmother's knee. She bit her bottom lip. "I like you, Gram. But back then I didn't know you at all. My parents never said anything nice about any of their parents. I guess I chose you because you were the only grandparent I could trace. I'm ashamed to say that now."

Gram patted the top of Maddy's head, looking into the distance as if she could see right through the Christmas tree.

Maddy continued. "I woke up when I became a Christian. I realized that there was more to life than parties and stuff. I decided I had to change my whole direction and go to college. I knew my parents wouldn't be any help. So my only hope was to find you and see if you'd be willing to have me." She sighed. "You don't hate me now, do you?"

Gram smiled at her and ruffled her hair. "I think you are terrific, Maddy MacDonald. I'm proud to know you."

"Then why don't you get close to me?"

Gram looked at the photo album again. "You are a free spirit Maddy. If I give my heart to you, you will take it with you when you leave and never look back."

Maddy opened her mouth to protest, then closed it when she remembered all the people she had promised to write, promised to keep in touch with. After she moved, her new life always took over, and she never did look back. Only once, she wrote a postcard to a friend in the fifth grade. Now, she couldn't even remember the girl's name.

"It hurts too much," Gram said. "I loved your father. I raised him. I poured heart and soul into him. And then, one day...." She turned her head away.

"Why did he leave?"

Gram looked at Maddy. "Do you really want to know?"

Maddy nodded.

"If I tell you, you may not want to stay with your old Gram anymore."

Gram sat herself next to Maddy on the sofa, reached for the photo album, and opened it. The first photo was of a woman in a brown tweed suit, holding a child wrapped in a blanket. "We didn't allow pictures to be taken when we were pregnant," she explained. "And never too soon after the baby was born. Sex was a taboo subject, and therefore, pregnancy with it. And me, I was supposed to be ashamed because of my circumstances."

Maddy stared at the young woman in the photo. So like herself. A smile from ear to ear. The skirt a little too tight. A little too short. "You weren't married," Maddy stated, hoping it would help her Gram to continue if she didn't sound like she was freaking out.

"No. I wasn't. I could say I made a mistake, and in front of God, it was nothing but blatant sin. But at that time, in my mind, I didn't know God very well. I figured he'd disapprove of anything I did anyway, so why bother worrying what he would think? Well, I truly loved Paul. He was your father's father."

"What happened to him? Why didn't you get married?"

"He was as flighty as I was. We'd talked about it, or I would never have gone to bed with him. When he found out I was pregnant, he couldn't stand the thought of being tied down so he disappeared. I haven't heard from him since."

"And Grandpa?"

She smiled sweetly. "The dearest man I've ever known."

"Better than Paul?"

Gram gave a tinkly chuckle. "Paul was a wisp of a lover's dream. Gorgeous, fun, full of life, but he had the fatal flaw of loving himself most of all. God was looking out for me when Paul left. As I said on Thanksgiving, I was pretty brazen to approach your grandfather like that. Later he said he looked into my eyes and knew that underneath was a woman whom he could live with and love for the rest of his life."

"Did he?"

"Oh my, yes. And his love for your father could not have been deeper if they had been blood related. Here, look at this...." In the photograph stood a tall, beaming man, wearing a black suit and a fedora. In one hand, he held his wife's, in the other, a young boy's. The next photograph showed the same man in the same suit, rolling around in the grass with the boy scrambling on top of him.

Gram turned the pages of the album. In page after page, the young boy grew. Birthday cakes with additional candles. Sports events. School events. In many of them, the tall man was somewhere. Or Gram was there. Gram told story after story about her little Toddy.

Maddy sat, mesmerized by the photos and stories. A whole

new world with her father in it. She saw him being raised in Seattle, watched the city grow with him.

"He looks so happy," Maddy said. "What happened?"

Gram sighed deeply. "I was a foolish woman, Maddy. I was, by that time, a woman with a deep faith in God. I was quite ashamed of my past and the fact that it had taken me so long to confess my sin. I didn't want my son to know what a terrible thing I had done. I didn't know where his father had gone. I couldn't even remember what he looked like, except that he had dark hair and dark eyes. It had been too many years since I had put that behind me.

"Todd was a teenager by then. Seventeen. Rowdy. Unfocused. He had one passion over all things—"

"Art," Maddy said.

"Yes. He drew without stopping on some days. He began to go down to the waterfront and draw people as they ate their meals. He drew the ships, the ferries, the birds. He wanted to go to Europe for his graduation. His father and I...I mean, stepfather...."

"That's okay, Gram. I understand."

"We had earned enough money to send him. But he needed a passport. And for his passport he needed an original birth certificate. I tried to do everything myself, but he found it."

Gram trembled a little and took a sip of tea. "He blew up. He felt so betrayed. Especially by Shawn—your grandfather. It was a terrible scene. Days of terrible scenes. Shawn tried to stay calm. He did most of the time. But the words Todd used, the things he said, were horrible, hurtful. He attacked me and what I had done. No amount of apology helped. Shawn reminded

Todd of his promise to do the portraits for the new library. Todd only screamed, 'It's a trick to make me stay. You don't care about me or my talent. You just want me to stay.'"

"And then?"

"He left. He never looked back. He called a couple times when you were born. Once in awhile your mother would call to say you were all right, but that there really was no point in us getting together." She was silent for a moment. "You know why your father draws portraits, don't you Maddy?"

Maddy shook her head.

"When he left, he said he was going to find his real father. He was going to travel the country. And when he drew the portrait of his father, he would know it. He's looking in malls everywhere, hoping to find his father." Gram took another sip of tea and stared into the fire. "He had a loving, wonderful father right here. But he couldn't be satisfied with that. Oh, I am so sorry I did not tell him when he was young that he was adopted."

"It's strange, Gram, but you talk about a library. Growing up, whenever I asked Daddy if we could go into a library, he always said, 'Why should we follow the foolish dreams of old men? It will only lock us in and make us stay.' Does that have to do with the library he was supposed to do portraits for?"

"Oh, my," Gram said, setting her teacup and saucer on the coffee table. "He wouldn't even let you go inside a library?"

Maddy shook her head.

Gram picked up the photo album. "Your grandfather's dream was to build a library. A place so beautiful, and so full of books, that people would come from all over to grow in knowledge. A place where people could come and see how words come to life."

Maddy nodded eagerly.

"And so he worked hard. He raised funds, he used all our own savings, he hired an architect and worked steadily with him. He even hired a wood carver to make the doors enticing.

"He surrounded the building with tall, wide windows so the building would be full of light. He made the inside so all the four stories of books could be seen from the main entrance, enticing people to come in and explore further. It was his dream. And for a long time, Todd was just as excited. When he discovered the truth about his birth, he vowed he would never set foot in a library again. He knew it would hurt your grandfather to the core of his being. And it did. Shawn nearly did not complete the library because of it."

"Is the library complete?"

Gram looked astonished. "You mean you don't know?"

"I guess not."

"MacDonald Library, sweetie."

Maddy looked blank.

"The library at PCU, the one you work in. That is your grandfather's library."

19

M addy stared at her grandmother.

"Shawn always hoped that one day, one of his grand-children would return to the library and love it as he did."

Maddy stood, and walked to the fire. "It doesn't say 'MacDonald Library' anymore. It looks like the old sign fell off and they haven't fixed it properly."

"Well, they had better!" Gram shook her head emphatically. "I'm very proud of the fact that my Shawn built that library."

Maddy collapsed in the wing chair. "I can't believe it."

Gram lifted the photo album and showed Maddy the rest of the pictures. The library in stages. Its growth. In some of the pictures Todd worked alongside Shawn. In a later group photo, his countenance had changed to anger. He stood with his arms crossed and glared at the camera while everyone else in the group smiled.

"This is amazing, Gram. I can hardly believe it."

Gram nodded. "Sometimes I go to the campus just to sit in the library. It makes me feel closer to Shawn than going to the cemetery."

Gram motioned toward the tree. "Come on. Open your presents. The day is passing."

Maddy didn't move. "You have given me so much already. Do you realize what a gift these pictures are to me? It is the first time I have ever seen any pictures of my family."

Gram nodded. "Just looking at them reminds me there were happy days. I can hold Shawn and Todd in my arms as I look at the photos."

"Pictures are important, aren't they?" Maddy said.

"They root you in time and place. They give you a history. They provide something to hold on to when the rest of life seems to be too chaotic. When you don't have a home, they give you a home to go to." Gram waved impatiently. "Now go. Before I have to get up on these arthritic hips and complain, so you feel guilty."

Maddy sat by the tree and reached underneath.

"That one last," Gram said when Maddy took a smallish, odd-shaped package.

"This one?"

Gram nodded.

Maddy took the paper off an oblong thing. "A photo album," Maddy said, trying to sound happy.

"You don't have any pictures, do you?"

"No."

"We'll have to change that. Now open the next one."

A rectangular box felt semiheavy. Maddy opened it carefully. She was afraid to believe what she saw on the cover of the box. She held her breath, reached in, and pulled out a camera. "Gram!" she shrieked. She ran to her grandmother and threw her arms around her. "I can't believe it. My own camera. Are you sure?"

Gram nodded, her eyes filled with tears. "I want you to have your own memories, Maddy. I want you to have a place to come home to. Maybe pictures will help with that."

The last package was a box with ten rolls of film. "Shoot 'em up," Gram said. "Don't be thrifty. You won't learn to take good shots unless you take a lot. I'll develop every single roll of film you shoot."

Maddy skimmed through the directions. When she was done, she looked at her Gram. "There's only one thing that would make this day perfect."

"What's that?"

"Get dressed and I'll tell you."

In a flash, they were both changed and ready to go. "Will you let me drive, Gram?"

Maddy got behind the wheel and carefully maneuvered the car down the street. She hadn't driven much, so was extra cautious. It didn't take long, since the streets were nearly deserted. She parked the car. "Please come with me, Gram."

They walked hand in hand up the sidewalk. When they got to MacDonald Library, Maddy had her grandmother sit on the wide cement platform next to the steps. They giggled like little schoolgirls as Maddy posed her grandmother. "You are the best," she whispered in her ear, then kissed her cheek. "I won't leave you, I promise." Maddy stepped back and aimed her camera. Gram smiled the truest, deepest, happiest smile Maddy had ever seen.

Maddy handed Gram the camera and walked past her up

the stairs. She put her fingers out to trace the lions carved in the massive front door. *Someone did put their heart and soul into this place.*

And that heart and soul is part of mine.

N U M B E R 1
FRESHMAN BLUES

By Wendy Lee Nentwig
ISBN 0-88070-947-2

Emily Stewart has looked forward to her freshman year at PCU for years. But things don't go quite as planned. When Emily's best friend loses her financial aid, Emily finds herself rooming instead with a sloppy New Yorker named Cooper. Not only that, but Em has to deal with her over-protective brother (who decides to date Cooper!), peer pressure, new friends, and college deadlines...not to mention inedible dorm food.

Further complications arise when Emily meets what may be the man of her dreams. At first, John Wehmeyer seems to be exactly the type of guy she has been waiting for: gorgeous, romantic, and a Christian! Best of all, John thinks that Emily is wonderful, too. But when conflicts arise, Emily learns the hard way that true love is about more than romance.

Yet, even as a frightening and climactic confrontation leaves her stranded far from campus, Emily makes exciting discoveries about herself and rediscovers an incredible source of strength that will see her through her *Freshman Blues* and beyond.

Available at your local Christian bookstore.
If it is not in stock, ask them to special order it for you!

N U M B E R 3
TRUE IDENTITY

By Bernie Sheahan
ISBN 0-88070-949-9

Kenzie Dawson, the Nashville-born-and-bred daughter of a Christian record company president, is using PCU as an escape from the pressures that come with being in the Christian music industry's inner circle. How long can she keep up the charade?

Kenzie finds that her reluctance to share the details of her Nashville life with her new PCU friends soon gets in the way. But it takes a budding romance with the musically talented Chris Gallagher, a Seattle concert appearance of longtime family friend and Christian pop star Billy Weber, and an ongoing tense relationship with Emily Stewart—her "Christian music freak" suitemate—to force Kenzie to make some difficult choices regarding the kind of person she wants to be.

Will she finally embrace her background, her Nashville life, and her own remarkable musical gifts? Or will she continue to hide the truth from her new friends, in hopes of creating a new image for herself, apart from her Nashville associations? Meet the real Kenzie Dawson in *True Identity*.

N U M B E R **4**
SPRING BREAK

By Wendy Lee Nentwig
ISBN 0-88070-950-2

Cooper Ellis's life is just beginning to come together. Looking for something
different, the ex-professional model has left her home in New York City for
college in the beautiful Pacific Northwest.

At school in Seattle she gets a great roommate and snags the guy of her
dreams, a starting guard on PCU's basketball team. But after six perfect
months together, her boyfriend starts having doubts about their relationship
and Cooper's spring break plans are turned upside-down. And it doesn't help
matters that just when her relationship is on the rocks, everyone around her
seems to be pairing up.

Forced to spend spring break far from her PCU friends, Cooper has a lot
of time to rethink her relationships, her decision to attend PCU, and her place
in the great, big world. But as she struggles with those questions, God shows
Cooper that in order to see his plan she didn't need to go all the way to
Seattle...she just had to open her eyes.

Available after September 1996 at your local Christian bookstore.
If it is not in stock, ask them to special order it for you!